Her Outdoors:

Risk, Challenge and Adventure

in Gendered Open Spaces

Edited by

Barbara Humberstone

LSA

Publication No. 66

First published in 2000 by
Leisure Studies Association

The collection as a whole © 2000 LSA
The individual contributions © 2000 the respective authors

A catalogue record for this book
is available from the British Library.

ISBN: 0 906337 76 3 ✓

Layout design and typesetting by Myrene L. McFee
Binding by Kensett Ltd., Hove

Contents

Risk, Challenge and Adventure and the Gendering of Open Spaces: Introduction

Barbara Humberstone

Buckinghamshire Chilterns University College, UK

The term 'outdoors' conjures up a variety of images and feelings, which depend upon the visionary and her/his practical, every day assumptions and theoretical and gendered positionings. As Crouch (1998: p. 11) muses, "countryside is not only 'outward' as intense ideological practice, or as 'gaze', but also part of enjoying something else, ... where particular traditions of land availability and regulation (state, commercial) make possible 'being around', being together, taking part in activities, events, in a group or alone. In the *doing*, aspects of 'environment', of countryside, mix with ways of being *in space*".

This doing and being in open space is not immune from — and it seems in considering 'the outdoor industry' only just beginning to engage with — analyses from a variety of perspectives such as cultural studies, Laconian psychoanalysis and its account of identity and subjectivity, various strands of feminism and Foucauldian concern with power and discourse. Such perspectives direct our attention to the notion that outdoor activities, participated in group or solo, are constructed not only by the material 'natural' environment but also through systems of meanings, by webs of power and through organisations and institutions that may provide their access and legitimisation (Humberstone *et al.*, 1998). Consequently, gender and difference are implicated in the constitution of doing and being in the outdoors. Gender conceptualised as "a pattern of relations among people ... an extensive and complex pattern woven through all institutions they live in ... and shapes their lives at every level" (Connell *et al.*, 1982: pp. 33–34) acknowledges its complexity and the implications of power. Recent feminist cultural geographical analyses have highlighted the importance of gender in developing theory related to space. Aitchison and Jordan's (1998) review of feminist analyses within the new cultural geography emphasises the

significance of this work for informing and developing our social understandings in relation to the gendering of spaces and places. In applying such
frameworks to the gendering of open 'outdoor' spaces, it may be possible to
explore whether the contestations or transformations are similar or different
from other leisured dimensions of society. Furthermore, we see Wearing
(1998: p. 181), in her critical feminist analyses of leisure theories, drawing
attention to the possibilities for women through some forms of leisure
activities and, referring to the outdoors, points to the women, 'who stretch
societally imposed limits on the use of the female body by engaging in
activities such as rock climbing and outdoor adventure (who) report a sense
of empowerment.' Wearing's review of empirical studies that take seriously the
experiences and meanings that women give to leisure, from the few studies of
outdoor adventure, suggests that the outdoors provides opportunities for
expanding the experiences of many women, although those cited are largely
only concerned with white mainly middle-class women in the USA. This
volume presents further empirical work from the UK, Australia and the
USA, but sadly it is concerned largely with white, able-bodied women. As
Collins in this volume emphasises, we have yet to hear the voices of
indigenous women, and 'other' women who may experience the outdoors from
very different perspectives.

   In addition to engaging with these social and cultural theories, social
conceptualisations of 'risk' are significant in furthering our understandings of
adventure in the outdoors. Much recent social commentary points to a
disintegrating of social solidarity of communities and the rise of individualism,
which arguably leaves the individual feeling disconnected, isolated and
vulnerable. Furthermore, it is proposed that as a consequence of the complex
processes of change, Western societies have developed a 'culture of fear',
leaving people feeling 'at risk' and unable to make decisions and take control.
Furedi (1997: p. 70) argues that "this lack of belief in the problem-solving
ability of human beings helps to heighten the sense of vulnerability". These
arguments lead one to believe that modern society is largely concerned with
risk avoidance and much of this discourse tends to ignore gendered dimensions. Voluntary engagement in risk-taking in the outdoors, solo and in groups,
in the context of a 'risk avoidance' society has not been explored to any degree
from critical sociological perspectives (but see Becker and Humberstone
forthcoming). Lyng (1990), however, suggests that risk taking through
adventurous activities, largely by men, is a consequence of modern societies'
control over individuals. The editor of *Adrenaline* magazine maintains that
extreme sport is a reaction "to more control in our lives, leading us to want
more risk"[1]. Furthermore, the media portray mainly men involved in risk-
taking adventurous activities in the outdoors and generally represent them as

'heroes'. When women do engage in these activities, sometimes with fatal consequences, they are depicted not as heroines, but behaving inappropriately and selfishly. This was the case for Alison Hargreaves, the British climber who having climbed a number of Himalayan peaks tragically died on K2 in 1995. The media were scathing of her for depriving her children of their mother. Such popular gendered responses and lack of attention to gendered outdoor spaces in social analyses is to a small extent addressed in this volume.

All of the contributions in this volume explore the experiences of women being outdoors, and the relations between open space, gender and risk/ challenge. The papers are informed by a variety of feminist perspectives and all are concerned to take seriously the subjectivities of women. But for that of Curson and Kitts, whose research is focused upon women's use of urban open spaces, the contributions are concerned with women engaged in doing specific 'adventurous' activities in open 'natural' environments.

Evans 1997, cited in Curson and Kitts in this volume, points to statistical evidence that "trends in leisure suggest a rapid growth in demand for outdoor, countryside and water based activities — adventurous and glamorous pursuits and new activities". Nature-based sport or activities no longer remain the interest of a few but are now identified as mass participative. Nevertheless, Anderson *et al.* (1996) in their survey of water-based provision in UK, found women and ethnic groups to be under-represented. Neither nature-based sports nor the use of nature-based adventurous activity as a 'vehicle for personal and social growth and development' is new, although the number of activities may have increased and the ideological justifications underpinning the traditional 'character building' notions of the outdoors changed[2]. What now is frequently loosely termed the 'outdoor industry' is generally assumed to include the provision of outdoor adventure education, which traditionally encompassed teaching and learning in 'wilderness' contexts or outdoor 'natural' spaces, and the more specific nature-based sport for its own sake. Clearly there is a blurring of boundaries between and amongst these phenomena. Traditional nature-based sport has a significant literary tradition, including writings of an autobiographical nature and much has also been written about the history and practice of outdoor adventure education, most of which written from male perspectives[3]. This notwithstanding, many such texts were largely written in splendid isolation with little engagement with social, cultural or geographical discourses. However, feminist critiques (e.g. Pedersen [1998] in Norway; Henderson and Bialeschki [1987] and Warren [1996] in USA) and other critical dimensions (e.g. Bowles, 1996; contributors to Higgins and Humberstone, 1998 and 1999), and those focusing upon important ecological perspectives (for example, Cooper, 1996; Higgins, 1996; Humberstone, 1998; Pedersen, 1993; Vanreusel, 1996) have recently emerged[4].

All the research undertaken to inform the papers in this volume is itself informed by feminist discourse. But for Curson and Kitts, each is a consequence of the researchers' personal and group experiences. The particular commitment to the phenomena identified by those doing adventurous activities in the outdoors is something shared by many involved in this sort of leisure/work/education. This can be both negative and positive for its understanding, as much previous research has been functionalist in approach, attempting to show uncritically that outdoor adventure is a 'good' thing. **Tony Curson and Clare Kitts**'s paper, 'Women's Use and Perception of the Outdoors: A Case Study of Urban Parks' (pp. 1–28), does not emerge largely as a consequence of the authors' experience but rather as part of a larger scale research project. It provides an important complement to the empirical interpretative research based upon the researchers' experiences that predominates in this collection. There are considerable benefits to the latter form of research as these do provide considerable insight into the lived experiences of women (see Clarke and Humberstone, 1997). It is equally important that we understand the open space leisure needs of urban women who may not have easy access to 'countryside' and/or 'waterside' and may not have the opportunity to voice their concerns, feelings and needs (Collins, 1999 ; Spratt et al., 1998). This is addressed by Curson and Kitts paper which uses a variety of techniques for collecting information concerning women's perceptions and use of parks in London. Clearly highlighted are the structural, inter-/intra- and subjective constraints on these women's leisure. They remain in a locality close to home, utilising the park not necessarily for their own leisure but to provide for children's needs. Fear limits women's use of urban parks, but some ways have been found for overcoming this and gaining access. The paper emphasises the socio-cultural dimensions and implications for future leisure policy, planning and management strategies.

Influenced by data emerging from ongoing research, **Di Collin**'s paper "Recognising Women: Discourses in Outdoor Education" (pp. 29–36) reflects upon the white, male discourses that dominate outdoor education ideology and practice world wide. Linking outdoor and environmental education, Collins highlights feminist critiques emerging in the environmental field, and draws attention to the invisibility not only of white women, but also Black, Asian and non English speaking women in the policy and practice of outdoor education.

The next four papers focus broadly upon women's involvement in making available outdoor adventure. In "Gender Issues and Women's Windsurfing" (pp. 37–50), **Val Woodward**, herself an enthusiastic windsurfer, provides insights into the experiences of women attending the windsurfing sessions that she teaches. Her feminism informs the ways in which she challenges dominant normalising discourses reinforced by some of the male providers at the lake in Cornwall, UK where she teaches. Through qualitative interpretive research and feminist praxis, Woodward uncovers interesting insights into the lived realities of the women participants and identifies beneficial strategies for leisure policy and practice.

A life-history research approach is taken by **Linda Allin** in her paper "Women into Outdoor Education: Negotiating a Male-gendered Space — Issues of Physicality" (pp. 51–68), examining the careers of women who have opted to work as teachers in the 'outdoor industry' in UK. She explores how the women relate to their physical selves, their family lives and the tensions engendered in negotiating both their identities and their capabilities within the male dominated outdoor career. **May Carter,** who contributes "Developing Confidence in Women Working Outdoors: An Exploration of Self Confidence and Competence in Women Employed in Adventure Recreation" (pp. 69–82), has also worked as a teacher in the outdoors and set up her own enterprise to provide adventure recreation in Australia. As a consequence of her experiences as a woman leader and manager in this male dominated arena, she felt compelled to research further the attitudes and practices that exist within the adventure recreation industry in Australia and the effects these have on the perceptions of women and on women's place within the industry. Differences in approaches between females and males are identified and, although there are exceptions, her paper, like Allin's, highlights the ways in which women's abilities and contributions as instructors are undermined and undervalued. Carter suggests that in the adventure recreation industry there appear contradictions between philosophy and practice which for many women excludes and undermines.

Karen Barak, Mary Anne Hendrich and Steven J Albrechtsen describe a model for enhancing self esteem in adolescent girls through adventure education programming in the USA in their contribution "Enhancing Self-esteem in Adolescent Girls: A Proposed Model for Adventure Education Programming" (pp. 83–100). Underpinned by feminist psychological analyses, this paper describes various adventurous activities and experiences and identifies key related elements for consideration in this experiential process. They go on to identify such elements as 'learning', 'risk' and 'facilitation' and suggest how best to provide beneficial experiences for young women. The final paper, "Gendered 'Natural' Spaces: a Comparison of Contemporary Women's Experiences of Outdoor Adventure (UK) and Friluftsliv (Norway)" (pp. 101–112) by **Barbara Humberstone and Kirsti Pedersen** is a feminist comparative analysis, highlighting not only gender dimensions but also environmental aspects of the outdoors.

These papers go some way to illuminating the gendering of the inter-linking leisure/work/educational dimensions of open 'natural' spaces.

Notes

[1] The magazine focuses upon extreme adventure sport. Comments on BBC Radio 4, PM at 5pm on 28th July 1999.

[2] Cook (1999: p. 172) makes an historical analysis of outdoor education and UK education legislation pointing to its gendered nature. The local government act of 1989 and its effect on the outdoor education provision in UK is discussed in Humberstone (1995)

[3] The outdoor industry has, in some sense, been dominated by the male traditions and ideologies of the 'Outward Bound' and arguably there has been little recognition of cultural difference (cf Becker forthcoming). Mortlock (1984) provides an alternative philosophy but still without awareness of difference.

[4] There is also some work that explores the phenomena as a construction of modernity. Whilst many outdoor education commentators would set themselves apart from the bungy jumping, quick adrenaline rush activities, 'commercialised' experience and so forth, critical analyses over a wide spectrum of phenomena are now beginning to emerge from a variety of perspectives.

References

Aitchison, C. and Jordan, F. (eds) (1998) Editors' introduction, *Gender, space and identity* (LSA Publication No. 63). Eastbourne: Leisure Studies Association, pp. v–ix.

Anderson, J., Andrews, R., Edwards, C., Harris, I., and Saville, T. (1996) *Natural Youth Water Sports Audit.* Southampton Institute and the British Marine Industries Federation.

Becker, P. (forthcoming) 'Desire, rejection or simply tolerance. How to find the adequate response to unfamiliar differences?', in European Institute for Outdoor Adventure Education and Experiential Learning, *European Perspectives in Outdoor Education.* Penrith: Cumbria: Adventure Education

Becker, P. and Humberstone, B. (eds)(in progress) *Adventure, nature and the outdoors: Against fragments of modernity.* London: Macmillan Press.

Bowles, S. (1996) 'Techniques and philosophy. Blending roots or sowing seeds in outdoor adventure education', *Journal of Adventure Education and Outdoor Leadership* Vol. 13, No. 2: pp. 7–13.

Clarke, G. and Humberstone, B. (1997) *Researching women and sport.* London: Macmillan Press.

Collins, D. (1999) 'Women youth workers and outdoor education', in P. Higgins and B. Humberstone (eds) *Outdoor education and experiential learning.* Luneburg, Germany: Verlag Erlebnispadagogik.

Connell, W, Ashenden, D., Kessler, S. and Dowsett, G. (1982) *Making a difference: Schools, families and social divisions.* Sidney: Allen and Unwin.

Cook, L. (1999) 'The 1944 Education Act and outdoor education: from policy to practice', *History of Education* Vol. 28, No. 2: pp. 157–172.

Cooper, (1996) 'The role of outdoor and field study centres in education for the 21 st Century', *Journal of Adventure Education and Outdoor Leadership,* Vol. 8, No. 2: pp. 10–11.

Crouch, D. (1998) 'Countryside at leisure', *Leisure Studies Association Newsletter,* No. 50 (July); p. 11.

Evans, G. (1997) *Trends in outdoor pursuits.* London: CELTS for Health Education Authority, University of North London.

Furedi, F. (1997) *Culture of fear. Risk-taking and the morality of low expectations.* London: Cassell.

Hendersen, K.A. and Bialeschki, D. (1987) 'Qualitative evaluation of a women's week experience', *Journal of Experiential Education,* Vol. 10, No. 6: pp. 25–29.

Higgins, P. (1996) 'Connection and consequence in outdoor education', *Journal of Adventure Education and Outdoor Leadership* Vol. 13, No. 2: pp. 34–39.

Higgins, P. and Humberstone, B. (eds) (1998) *Celebrating diversity: Learning by sharing cultural differences.* Buckinghamshire: European Institute for Outdoor Adventure Education and Experiential Learning.

Higgins, P. and Humberstone, B. (eds) (1999) *Outdoor education and experiential learning in the UK.* Luneburg, Germany: Verlag Erlebnis-padagogik.

Humberstone, B. (1995) 'Commercialisation of outdoor education — profit and loss in adventure', in L. Lawrence, E. Murdoch and S. R. Parker (eds) *Professional and development issues in leisure, sport and education.* LSA Publication No. 56. Eastbourne: Leisure Studies Association, pp. 135–146.

Humberstone, B. (1998) 'Re-creation and Connections in and with Nature: Synthesizing Ecological and Feminist Discourses and Praxis?', *International Review for the Sociology of Sport* Vol. 33, No. 4, pp. 381–392.

Humberstone, B., Amesberger, G., Becker, P., Bowles, S., Higgins, P., Keus, B., Neuman, J. and Schirp, J. (1998) 'Culture, diversity, national communities and outdoor adventure education', in P.Higgins and B.Humberstone (eds) *Celebrating diversity: Learning by sharing cultural differences*. Buckinghamshire: European Institute for Outdoor Adventure Education and Experiential Learning.

Lyng, S. (1990) 'Edgework: A social psychological analysis of voluntary risk taking', *American Journal of Sociology*, Vol. 95, No. 4: pp. 851–85.

Mortlock, C. (1984) *The adventure alternative*. Milnethorpe, Cumbria: Cicerone Press.

Pedersen, K. (1993) 'Gender, nature and technology: Changing trends in 'wilderness life' in northern Norway', in R. Riewe and J. Oakes (eds) *Human Ecology: Issues of the North* Vol. 11. Edmonton: Canadian Circumpolar Institute, University of Alberta, pp. 33–66.

Pedersen, K. (1998) 'Doing feminist ethnography in the 'wilderness' around my hometown: Methodological reflections', *International Review for the Sociology of Sport* Vol. 33, No. 4: pp. 393–402.

Spratt, G., McCormack, J. and Collins, D. (1998) 'The Discovery Project: A perspective from the UK', in P. Higgins and B. Humberstone (eds) *Celebrating diversity: Learning by sharing cultural differences*. Buckinghamshire: European Institute for Outdoor Adventure Education and Experiential Learning.

Vanreusel, B. (1995) 'From Bambi to Rambo: Towards a socio-ecological approach to the approach to the pursuit of outdoor sports', in O. Weiss and W. Schulz (eds) *Sport in space and time*. Vienna: Vienna University Press. pp. 273–282.

Warren, K (eds)(1996) *Women's voices in experiential education*. Dubuque, Iowa: Kendall/Hunt

Wearing, B. (1998) *Leisure and feminist theory*. London: Sage.

Women's Use and Perceptions of the Outdoors: A Case Study of Urban Parks

Tony Curson and Clare Kitts

Centre for Leisure and Tourism Studies, University of North London (UK)

Introduction

Increasing attention is being paid to the role and use of urban parks due to cut backs in public expenditure, concern about the quality of experience offered by these facilities, their educational and social potential and the economic benefits of providing parks as key image creators and tourist attractions for towns and cities. There is increasing analysis of the gendered nature of many leisure environments and activities (e.g. Wimbush, 1986; Green, Hebron and Woodward, 1987; Deem, 1986; Hargreaves, 1994) but there is a limited, albeit growing (e.g. Scraton and Watson, 1998), body of knowledge regarding women's use and perceptions of the outdoor environment in urban contexts for leisure. A similar pattern of limited coverage of leisure opportunities and participation has until recently been observed in the geographical study of women in the urban environment which has tended to be economic in nature (e.g. Massey, 1984). Bondi (1992), McDowell (1990) and Valentine (1989; 1992) are representative of increasing attention to feminist issues within geography broadly. Hence this paper attempts to present some recent research findings on women's perceptions and use of parks in London whilst drawing on findings from previous research in the areas of leisure studies, feminist geography, cultural studies and planning. The paper aims to identify some of the factors influencing women's perceptions of urban parks as leisure environments with reference to the social construction of place. The issue of women's fear in the urban environment has previously been identified as having significance with respect to outdoor leisure activities (e.g. Burgess, Harrison and Limb, 1988) and this is also identified in our research. The policy, planning and management implications of the research findings will be

1

discussed in order to contribute to the debate over the relative public, accessible nature of public open spaces.

Trends in leisure

It is necessary to observe briefly some of the trends in the use of the outdoor environment for leisure and usage of urban parks by women. A review of GHS data, Sports Council and Social Trends studies carried out by Evans (1997) suggests that the British population is becoming more active, with rapid growth in demand for outdoor, countryside and water based activities particularly those associated with healthy lifestyles, adventurous and glamorous pursuits and new activities. Major growth areas are non-competitive and individual pursuits and those offering flexible programming. Men and women are becoming more active although the gender difference is still marked with women participating less often than men. This is evident in trends for walking which continues to be the most popular outdoor activity. However, active pursuits are still minority activities with home-based, passive pastimes dominating our leisure.

It is generally accepted that people tend to participate more often in leisure activities available close to home and this is especially true for those with restricted mobility such as women who are more likely to have to rely on public transport, making journeys more time consuming and less convenient, particularly if children are being accompanied (Williams, 1995). When viewed in combination with the fact that women are amongst those less likely to have access to rural open spaces (Glyptis, 1991), it is not surprising to note that parks, as relatively local facilities, are one of the main outdoor amenities for many urban women. However, use of urban parks has generally declined in the UK in parallel with local authority expenditure cutbacks and CCT (Compulsory Competitive Tendering) of their maintenance and operation since 1988. Despite this, their value is still recognised in terms of providing space for passive and peaceful recreation for local residents in addition to their ecological and environmental functions (Williams, 1995, Evans, 1997).

Women's leisure

It is widely recognised that women's lives are constrained differently to men's and, as a social entity, leisure is directly influenced. It is outside the scope of this paper to discuss women's 'relative freedoms' (Wimbush and Talbot, 1988) in detail. But, in summary, the constraints presenting women with a more narrow leisure experience can be described as being structural, inter-personal and intra-personal. Structural constraints operate at the societal level and overall could be seen to be the result of the western patriarchal society which perpetuates the role of women primarily as home makers and child carers above other roles they may endeavour to establish. This has a cyclical impact in ensuring male domination of the economy and possibly the world outside the home, whilst women tend to remain in the locality of the home. Inter-personal constraints refer to the role of the woman as carer and companion which indicates that women are less likely than men to pursue an activity for intrinsic purposes. For example, the mother who takes her child to the local park is deemed to be involved in a leisure activity but possibly not one of her own choosing, rather undertaking a parental duty of providing the child with fresh air and space in which to run. Intra-personal constraints refer to the influence of other people's views in women's choice of leisure activities. For example, in sporting terms, women are encouraged to participate in feminine appropriate sports such as netball, gymnastics or dance (Hargreaves, 1994) rather than those typically associated with men such as rugby or boxing. "It cannot be assumed that all women experience the outdoors in a similar way" (Henderson *et al.*, 1996: p. 190), but as a generalisation, it can be claimed that in the outdoors these structural, inter- and intra-personal constraints on women's leisure operate in unison to create differing patterns of perceptions and use of urban parks for men and women.

Previous research on women and urban parks

Until comparatively recently, there had been little research in the UK into general user behaviour and attitudes, and even now there have been few studies which have drawn out the issues for women. This is surprising given the importance of parks as features of the urban landscape. In the last two decades, however, there have been a number of studies which have defined patterns of use in parks. These have included a report by the Tourism and Recreation Research Unit (TRRU) (Walker and Duffield, 1983), a study in the Potteries in Staffordshire by Williams and Jackson (1985), a study of open spaces in Greenwich by Burgess *et al.* (1988), and a number of surveys by park authorities such as Milton Keynes (1988, 1995a), Newham (reported in Page *et al.*, 1994), Bexley (reported in LBA, 1995). More recently, Comedia / Demos (1995) carried out both empirical and observational research as part of their 'Parklife' study. All these studies have revealed gender contrasts in park use, although the differences are not always consistent. Most studies have shown less use by women overall, although this depends on the size of the catchment (more local parks attract more women), nature of the facilities (e.g. playgrounds attract mothers/children whilst sports facilities attract more men), ease of access and other factors. Fear seems to have become a constraint on women's use of parks in recent years. Few studies have highlighted the difference between men and women in the behavioural patterns in park use. Burgess *et al.* (1988) is an exception in which the social dimension to park use for many women is contrasted with their common use by men for solitude or functional purposes. In Milton Keynes, focus groups research (Milton Keynes Parks Trust, 1995) was used to identify the particular perspectives and concerns of women, which has led on to management and promotional strategies aimed at securing more women's use of parks; whilst earlier research in the Royal Parks (Richards and Curson, 1993) showed that women's use of parks was disproportionately influenced by the weather, by the demands of children, by ease of access and by special activities and events.

Space, place and gendered landscapes

Urban parks usually appear on maps as bland two dimensional patches of green ink which belies the depth of experience and meaning endowed on and generated by such spaces. Increasingly the variety of social meanings imbued on parks rather than their physical design and operation has attracted the attention of researchers.

Space is objective but place is a social construction so that one objective space has a variety of realities (Lowenthal, in Walmsley and Lewis, 1993) despite being products of common cultural and symbolic elements and processes. Such fusing of the objective and subjective elements has been described as resulting in Lifespace (Lewin, 1936, in Walmsley and Lewis, 1993) or Lifeworlds (Simmons, 1993) in which each individual operates.

Massey (in Keith and Pile, 1993: p. 156) states that "space is by its very nature full of power and symbolism, a complex web of relations of domination and subordination of solidarity and co-operation... kind of 'power-geometry'" as it is conceptualised and created out of social relations. Indeed, Relph (1976: p. 1) suggests that "To be human is to live in a world that is filled with significant places" but also that "to be human is to have and to know your place".

Relph continues to assert the male domination of landscape in his later comment (1976: p. 3) that "places have meaning: they are characterised by the beliefs of man". Additionally, Rapoport (1982) believes that "all landscapes are symbolic" and that this serves to establish and reinforce the values of dominant groups in society. For example, the construction of parks as landscapes of fear for some women may be construed to be a form of patriarchal social control.

Urban planning and the various agencies which have been responsible for developing and managing parks, such as local authorities and the Royal Parks Agency, have been dominated by men and thus could be seen to be part of the dominant culture of patriarchy. For example, Greed (1996a: p. 573) claims that "the British planning system often appears to act as a barrier to those seeking to make urban areas more accessible to women, the elderly, those responsible for child care and the disabled". In addition, she claims that "There has been relatively little specific consideration of women's leisure needs in contrast to the immense amount of land, money and effort which has been devoted to playing fields and sports centres used primarily by men" (op cit: p. 259) and women also tend to be viewed as equivalent to children when provision of facilities and management of parks are being considered (Greed, 1994). Despite this, Greed recognises that more consideration needs to be given to women with children. Bondi (1992) discusses Jenck's (1978) work claiming the predominance of masculine images of superiority in the urban environment. One only has to look at the monuments and statues within London's parks to notice the lack of female icons and what may be interpreted as phallic symbols (Wearing and Wearing, 1996). Numerous authors have entered into the debate regarding the ability of landscapes to communicate cultural messages. The 'new' cultural geographers, Cosgrove and Daniels (1988) view landscapes as ways of seeing rather than objective realities and Jackson (1989) also provides a critique of landscape geography, politicising culture whilst viewing it as having causal powers in framing how we view the world. With specific reference to tourist activities, Urry (1995) perceives the demand to 'gaze' as a socially constructed, cultural desire. It is this unnatural phenomena which he later developed, providing a sociology of place based around concerns over the production of places and their visual consumption in both the natural and built environment. With particular reference to gendered messages communicated with the environment, Duncan (1996) focuses on contemporary cultural studies and social theory and Mowl and Towner (1995) and Green (1998), amongst others, who looked at leisure more generally have progressed the debate.

Cosgrove (in Gregory and Walford, 1989: p. 126) talks of dominant landscapes being prominent suggesting that "despite the passage of time... [English parks] ... symbolise ideals of decency and propriety held by Victorian bourgeoisie" which helps to maintain the historical dominant values. He also suggests that alternative landscapes exist including the landscape of the excluded, which may include women. Pollard's Pastoral Interludes photographic exhibition in 1984 illustrated how as a black woman she feels that she does not belong in the countryside and feels threatened by the predominantly white visitors and the culturally produced landscape.

Cloke and Little (1997) develop this idea in Contested Countryside Cultures focusing on 'otherness'. Cosgrove suggests (op cit: p. 133) that "the organisation and use of space by women presupposes a very different set of symbolic meanings than by men, and in the past decade some important beginnings have been made in revealing the significance of gender in the attribution and reproduction of landscape symbolism". Wilson (1991) supported this notion suggesting that women represented feeling, sexuality and chaos whilst men represented rationality and control. She suggests that although the notion of city culture has developed as one pertaining to men, within this women present a threat firstly because in the city women are freer, despite the dangers, to escape the rigidity of patriarchal social controls which can be so powerful in a smaller, rural community and, secondly, women have seemed to represent disorder in western visions of metropolis.

Thereby, the thrust of Keith and Pile's (1993) book, in common with Urry (1995) amongst others, is that place is political, it is not simply a geological phenomena. It is the complex, multi-dimensional nature of place that is important to our perceptions of places. Before going on to discuss one aspect of women's perceptions of urban parks, their image as 'hot spots' or 'fear generators' (Nelson, 1997), it is useful to discuss briefly the way in which the use of parks by women (and men) may be influenced by their perceptions of these places.

Perception, in its broadest sense, is a complex process which has been approached in detail by numerous commentators, such as psychologists, usually in relation to the detailed processes of cognition; geographers, such as Pocock (1993); planners such as Aitken and Rushton (1993); and sport, leisure and tourism researchers (e.g. Bale, 1989; Urry, 1990). Most of the latter groups recognise the major role that socialisation and cultural construction has on our perceptions of places, people and activities. Closely allied to perception is landscape evaluation which has long been a subject of debate within the discipline of geography and, within leisure studies, various authors have approached the subject with myriad foci. For example, early studies such as Penning-Rowsell's (1982) discussed the public preference approach, the habitat based approach is introduced and revisited by Appleton (1996) with concern for biological survival being the driving force and Urry (1990) has discussed the tourist gaze.

Tuan (1974) describes the development of affective ties with the material environment producing a sense of belonging to a place as topophilia. Eyles (1985, cited in Gregory and Walford, 1989) believes that such place attachment is important in our quality of life. Tuan (1977: pp. 144–5) described how "familiarity breeds affection when it does not breed contempt". These complex, positive socio-emotional capabilities of leisure landscapes such as parks are currently being utilised for the purposes of place boosting (Bale, 1992). Due to public sector financial constraints and the recognition of the role of urban parks in tourism generation and economic development, attention is increasingly focused on the image creating abilities of these urban resources.

Alternatively, places can develop topophobia whereby a space becomes an environment of resentment or fear. For example, Williams (1995: p. 1) felt that "urban poverty, unemployment, social stress, racial tensions, rising crime, and most of all, increases in the fear of crime, can be seen as potentially powerful impediments of widespread use of urban environments by people at leisure".

Ravenscroft in a paper presented to the Recreation in the City Conference (1995) suggested that fear of crime in urban open space was a result of a cultural shift from a public to private culture and the associated idea that groups with relative power will exert themselves by dominating territory. He suggests that weaker groups will respond by participating in deviant behaviour which may be perceived as dangerous. He also suggests that over-zealous management may be a cause of such deviancy.

In *Parklife*, Comedia (1995: p. 3) suggest that "the declining quality of Britain's urban parks and open spaces is now a matter of extensive public concern, and is part of a wider fear that we can no longer manage safety and well-being in public spaces". In addition, Pain (1997: p. 231) suggests that "fear of crime is a leading social and political concern in western cities and women's fear of male violence constitutes the core of the problem in terms of its quantity and nature". It is widely recognised that women fear violent crime more than men although crime statistics, despite their major limitations, show that men are much more likely to be victims. Pain (1997: p. 233) suggests that women have been shown to be more fearful for their personal safety which "reinforces dominant patterns of political relations" thus further constraining women's freedom of choice within leisure. Generally, women's fear in urban spaces has become a feature of debate within the planning profession in particular during the 1980s and 1990s (e.g. MATRIX, 1984, Women's Design Service, 1993).

Valentine (1989: p. 385) addressed the "relationship between women's fear of male violence and their perception and use of public space" and suggested that women's perceived risk of attack in the public arena is greater than reality and that women are more likely to become victims in their homes. However, such fears of public spaces are real so if public providers of parks are to make accessibility a reality, further consideration of these perhaps irrational fears is required. Valentine (1992) suggests that women are socialised to fear the outdoors and to take precautionary actions as a result as part of the process of male hegemony.

Mowl and Towner (1995: p. 104) state that "space is gendered both physically and perceptually" identifying the physical structure and layout of the built environment, male domination of the planning and decision making process, geographical gender divisions and individual perceptions as having significant influence. Pain (1991) indicates that the built environment has been shown to constrain women through its structure, architecture and stereotypical ideas about appropriate behaviour in certain places for men and women. For example, Rose (1993: p. 34) believes that "sexual attacks warn women every day that their bodies are not meant to be in certain places". Valentine (1992) suggests that four main processes operate to create and perpetuate such fears of certain public spaces; common experiences of women, the media, social contact and stereotypes. Pain (1997) also suggests that fear of crime is not static but that it is spatially, temporally and socially (including class, life stage, ethnicity) determined. Burgess, Harrison and Limb (1988: p. 466) described a core aspect of their Greenwich Open Space Project findings as the 'dark side of open spaces'; primarily women's anxieties and fear associated with open spaces which were underpinned by feelings of a collapse of community and the associated collective care and responsibility including teenage delinquency, male sexual violence against unaccompanied women, racial attack, child abuse and abduction. They commented that, "Sadly in many cases, the fears become dominant and people find themselves increasingly, unable to participate in the pleasures of being in urban green spaces" thus supporting a view that perception and behaviour are inter-related.

Burgess (1996) has undertaken further research into the fear of crime in recreational woodlands finding that fear is predominantly socially based rather than landscape specific. For example, the dominant fear of women was found to be sexual crime but others included getting lost, being out at dusk, risk to their small children, daughters and mothers. Men are more inclined to fear getting lost, fear of the dark and fears for female and young members of their families with robbery and male rape being more minor concerns.

Sharma (1993) found that minority ethnic groups, and especially women members, expressed fears for safety when using London Borough of Newham leisure facilities including parks. These fears tended to be focused on racist attacks and a perception that they were not welcome in the parks but Smyth and Pearlman (1995) also found that white users felt equally unsafe in parks in the Borough. They found that overall a lack of perceived safety was a deterrent to park use.

The women's fears in Burgess's study (1996) tended to be greatest in wooded areas which were also the most highly valued landscapes. The irony of the most valued landscapes being the most fearful is significant especially if one considers Appleton's (1996) belief that wooded areas can represent safe refuge. Pain (1997: p. 235) also suggests that it is "dark, lonely and unfamiliar places which women associate with the possibility of attack" which seem to have implications for the notion of parks or the countryside allowing users, especially women, to get away from it all.

In the context of the fear-generating qualities of car parks, Nelson (1997: p. 3) states that "Fear is accepted as influencing the spatial and temporal behaviour of individuals as they attempt to reduce their exposure to potential risk" so it is logical to suggest that those fearing parks as landscapes will develop coping strategies which may include avoiding using them or aspects of them at certain times. This is illustrative of the narrowing of women's freedom in leisure.

This brief review of the literature has shown that perceptions of open space can vary between men and women. The paper now moves on to explore the extent to which these differing perceptions are translated into different use patterns and attitudes towards urban parks in London and if so, what implications this has for park policy and planning.

Case studies

Two main pieces of research have provided the empirical data for this paper. The first was a major 3-year survey of the use of London's Royal Parks carried out on behalf of The Royal Parks Agency over the period 1994-1996 and the second was a visitor and household survey of the use of parks in the inner London Borough of Islington, carried out for the Borough Council during 1996-1997. Both studies were undertaken by the Centre for Leisure and Tourism Studies at the University of North London. Although there was a gender perspective to the surveys, particularly the Islington ones, they were not primarily designed to obtain information about women's use of parks. However, the surveys did reveal some interesting differences in use and attitudes between men and women and these are described in the following sections.

Research methods

Royal Parks

This study was designed to collect information on the use of, and attitudes towards, the nine Royal Parks (Regent's Park, Primrose Hill, St. James's Park, Green Park, Hyde Park, Kensington Gardens, Greenwich Park, Bushy Park and

Richmond Park). This followed the transfer of the Royal Parks to agency status in April 1993 and the necessity to establish performance indicators so that the objectives of the new Agency could be monitored. One of these indicators was visitor satisfaction. The Agency was also concerned to know what visitors thought of the parks and where improvements might be made. The study was an extension of, and a contribution to, the Royal Parks Reviews which were taking place over the same period under the chair of Dame Jennifer Jenkins. The research provided a unique opportunity to study the use of these parks, which are arguably some the most famous and prestigious in the world; and whilst they might not be typical examples of urban parks, they do, perhaps, provide models of good practice in park provision and management.

The Royal Parks study sought to discover and evaluate: the number of visits to the parks; the visitor profile of the parks; the motivation for and characteristics of the visit; and the impression of and satisfaction with the visit. The need to generate quantitative data on patterns of park use as well as information about the views of current park users dictated the use of an inter-view-based, on-site survey of park users. This was implemented by interviewing a random sample of visitors using a structured questionnaire, augmented by the use of a self-completion questionnaire to obtain a representative sample of certain minority groups. Estimates of the volume of visitor use were obtained via a series of visitor counts. Almost 20,000 questionnaires were completed in year one of the study. This sample size was designed to enable satisfaction levels to be estimated within +/− 2.5% with 95% confidence and permitted user activities and views to be analysed with statistical accuracy at a sub-group level. Known satisfaction levels from year one enabled the sample size to be reduced by 50% in year two (i.e. 10,000 interviews), whilst retaining the same confidence level and interval as well as providing a representative user profile. In year three a smaller survey of 2,500 was undertaken into specific aspects of provision and management. In combination, these surveys are thus the largest ever carried out in urban parks in the UK.

Interviews were conducted on eight days per park during the year, which normally comprised four weekdays, three weekend days and a bank holiday. This allowed for variations in the level and pattern of use to be accom-modated. Interview locations consisted of both exit gates and nodal points within the park. The counts included observation data on different visitor types which were used to weight the survey data.

Islington parks

The research undertaken for the London Borough of Islington stemmed from a desire by the Council to produce performance indicators for the Audit

Commission and to obtain feedback on the use of and attitudes towards the parks, in order to demonstrate their importance and justify investment decisions (and possibly seek National Lottery funding). Another motivation was the desire to find out specifically about women's use of and attitudes towards parks arising out of the Council's 'Women's Action Plan', in which this was raised as an issue. In addition, the Council was keen to obtain the views of non-users in order to attempt to assess the significance of parks within the wider community.

Public open space in Islington accounts for only 5.2% of the borough area and it ranks second last among the London boroughs, in front only of Kensington and Chelsea (Sayers, 1993). The Borough is also the most densely populated in the country (OPCS, 1993). In contrast with the Royal Parks, the parks and open spaces in Islington are modest in scale and character and consist mainly of town squares, gardens and small informal open spaces. Highbury Fields is the largest and most well known park in the borough. The Council had also reduced the parks budget in the preceding two years and, whilst some new investment had been made, many of the parks exhibited signs of long term under-resourcing. The research therefore presented different challenges in terms of the scale, profile and role of the parks and likely user perceptions.

The Islington Parks research sought to establish current usage patterns and satisfaction levels at a range of different parks and open spaces; to identify areas where there was dissatisfaction with the current service and obtain views on possible improvements; and to provide information on the use of the service as a means of demonstrating its value and to guide future planning. The research strategy consisted of two major components: an interview-based site survey using a structured questionnaire (including some limited head counts) and a postal survey of households in four polling districts in the borough also using a structured questionnaire. The parks chosen for the visitor survey were: Barnard Park, Finsbury Square, Gibson Square, Gillespie Park, Highbury Fields, King Henry's Walk, Wray Crescent and Woodfall Road. The parks varied in size from 0.3 acres to 29 acres with most of them being small in scale and containing a limited range of facilities. A total of 1,481 interviews were conducted across these eight parks which was sufficient to permit analysis at the sub-group level, that is comparisons between parks or between different groups of users. Interviewing took place on between 3 and 7 days per park over two one-month periods in winter/spring and summer. This covered a reasonable range of weather and usage patterns and allowed some comparison between different seasons.

The Islington household survey consisted of sending out 3,400 question-naires to a systematic random sample of residents in four polling districts in the borough chosen from the electoral register. The survey was conducted during May 1996. Postcard reminders were sent out three weeks after the original mailing to increase the response rate. The response rate was 23% resulting in 771 usable questionnaires.

In order to assess whether the interviewees were representative of park users as a whole both surveys monitored the sex of visitors, non-respondents and respondents. In the Islington parks, men and women were more or less equally willing to participate in the survey; whilst in the Royal Parks survey, there was a higher refusal rate among women.

This imbalance was corrected through appropriate weighting of the survey data to reflect the proportions of males and females in the head counts. Possible reasons for these different response rates, as well as relative usage patterns and attitudes between men and women are discussed below.

The data from both studies were analysed using SPSS. The data on women's use and attitudes towards the parks were extracted from the survey results and chi-squared tests and correlations were performed on the data to identify significant differences and relationships.

Profile of female visitors to parks

The Royal Parks and Islington's Parks provide a sharp contrast in terms of volume of use. Whilst it is estimated that 30 million visits per year are made to the Royal Parks (an average of 9, 000 visits per park per day), putting them near the top of the list of UK visitor attractions, the number of people using Islington's parks is low. Regular spot counts for Islington found an average of between 4 and 22 people in parks at any one time. Whilst these figures conceal wide variations in use between parks and time periods, they con- firmed the impressions gained whilst undertaking the surveys that the Royal Parks are usually busy, whilst Islington's parks are generally quiet and in some cases often deserted and desolate.

As mentioned earlier, previous surveys of park use have generally found that more women than men use parks. Our research, however, showed a bias towards male use of the parks (52% in the Royal Parks and 54% in Islington overall), which contrasts with both local and national population figures where women are in the majority. This reflects the gender imbalance in commuting, dog walking and other individual activities such as jogging which form the main activities in many of the parks we surveyed. Inner London parks in particular, are heavily used for functional purposes such as short- cuts to work, rather than recreational visits and these tend to be dominated by men. There is a small but significant increase in the proportion of female visitors in better weather, reflecting the recreational and family oriented purpose of discretionary visits. Females are particularly under-represented among younger and older visitors with only 40% of those under 16 and over 65 being female. Women in the 25-44 age group are particularly well represented. To the extent that sample sizes allowed, our research showed that parks tend to be used proportionately by all ethnic groups (including women from these groups), suggesting that parks do not present the barriers to multi-ethnic use which seem to apply to other types of leisure facilities such as sports centres.

Unsurprisingly, only one third of women were in full-time employment compared to over half of men. Approximately 12% of female visitors to the Royal Parks were retired and similar proportions were students and housewives. Over a quarter of women users of the Royal Parks were local workers, mainly either using the park as a pleasant route to or from work, or for a lunchtime break and this figure rises to over a third in Islington's parks. The catchment area for parks is more local for women than for men. Over half of female visitors to the Royal Parks live within one mile of the park, compared with only 41% of male visitors. These figures are even higher for Islington's Parks, where the corresponding figures are 69% and 61% respectively. Clearly, the difference in the catchments between the two sets of parks reflects their size, location and range of facilities available.

Characteristics of park use by women

Although urban parks function at a variety of levels, their prime significance as local amenities, particularly for women, is indicated by the method of travel used to get there. Approximately 40% of visits to the Royal Parks by women (and a similar proportion for men), were on foot. Islington's parks function even more clearly as local facilities with over three quarters of visits on foot (compared to 66% of visits by men). Less than 1% of women (compared with 7% of men) cycle to the park. This pattern of use is also reflected in the time that visitors spend in the park. Overall, visitors do not spend long in parks, although women stay longer than men. Over half of visits to Islington's parks are less than 15 minutes duration and 69% are less than half an hour. The average duration of visits to the Royal Parks is an hour, although this figure is skewed by relatively few long visits. The use of urban parks often reflects local patterns of movement, with nearly half of all visits in the case of Islington's parks being combined with other activities such as work, school or shopping. Over half of all visitors to these parks use the park daily, and even in the case of the Royal Parks, over a quarter of visits are made by daily users, the majority of whom are women. The importance of parks as local open spaces and recreational facilities for women is illustrated by results of the

Islington household survey which found that 53% of women visit their local park regularly and 34% do so occasionally. Furthermore, 45% of women visit other Islington parks regularly and 46% do so occasionally. As the location and distribution of facilities such as shops and public services has changed, however, with a move to the urban periphery (Marshall and Wood, 1995), and with an increasing number of local journeys made by car, personal activity patterns have changed, particularly for women, with potentially serious implications for the use of urban parks to add to the under- resourcing referred to earlier.

Previous research has identified that the primary use of parks is for informal, passive recreation within an environment that caters principally for quiet, restorative pursuits (e.g. Walker and Duffield, 1983) and that the most popular features of parks are the natural ones — wide open spaces, peace and quiet and green landscapes. Our surveys confirmed this, although individual parks — particularly some of the Royal Parks — exhibit a wide range of uses, and there were significant differences in the use of parks by men and women. Less women than men visit parks for peace and quiet, exercise and as a short cut, whereas more women visit for walking the dog and for bringing the children. There is a functional aspect to these latter activities, not only in terms of undertaking family and domestic responsibilities but also, as other research (e.g. Burgess *et al.*, 1988) has suggested, in providing a sense of security in what may be perceived as a potentially risky environment. Women also appear to be more sensitive than men to the aesthetic and ecological features of parks. A higher proportion of women reported observing or feeding wildlife whilst on their visit and appreciating the flora and fauna and countryside qualities of the park. There was also a slightly higher majority of women in favour of natural as opposed to formal park landscapes.

Several surveys have demonstrated the importance that people place on parks. The significance of the Royal Parks to Londoners — residents, local workers and commuters — was illustrated in the Department of the Environment's 'Ten Thousand Views of London', where parks scored the highest (72%) of the 'Top 20 best things about London'. Research in Milton Keynes (Curson, 1995a) also found that parks and open spaces were considered to be the best feature of the city, and that the quality of the environment was instrumental in attracting new businesses to the city. Our research confirmed the high value placed on parks, particularly for their convenience rather than for the specific characteristics of individual parks. This is consistent with other parks research (e.g. Williams and Jackson, 1985), which has shown that if the motives for visiting parks are simply to walk, sit and relax, play or walk the dog, then in selecting a location people do not draw a distinction between different types of open space; they visit the one that is nearest and most convenient. The household survey in Islington showed that this support for parks is not confined to those who visit them but that they have a significant option and existence value in addition to their use value.

Women appear to attach a more significant social value to parks than do men. This is manifest both in the way that they use and perceive these places. A higher proportion of women visit parks with family and friends (57% in the case of the Royal Parks and 48% in the case of Islington's parks), whereas more men visit on their own. Clearly, this is partly a result of the male bias in the incidental and functional use of parks for commuting, but also seems to reflect male preferences for peace and solitude and as an escape from the noise and pressure of urban life. Women, on the other hand have a greater propensity to see the park as a social venue to meet friends, take the children, picnic, sightsee and attend events. The exception to this is a male domination in the use of parks for sports activities. Having said this, the relatively high proportion of lone visits, particularly in the Islington study, which contrasts with previous research (e.g. Williams and Jackson, 1985), indicates that the parks may not be maximising their role as community facilities in the sense of providing shared experiences.

One of the main purposes of both surveys was to measure the degree of visitor satisfaction with the quality and 'performance' of the parks. This was done by asking respondents using a 'Likert'-type scale, to rate a number of features of the park such as cleanliness and maintenance, seats, toilets, refreshments, shelter, lighting, play facilities, nature conservation, inform-ation and events. Overall, satisfaction ratings were higher for the Royal Parks than for Islington's parks. Whilst a comparison between the two sets of parks is not entirely fair since they are very different in scale and character, visitors' different expectations will have influenced their responses to dampen the effect of this. Visitors to the Royal Parks were generally satisfied with the environment of the parks and their maintenance but less satisfied with cer-tain park facilities such as toilets, shelter, lighting and information/signing. Similar concerns about park facilities were evident in Islington, in addition to more negative comments about the landscape/maintenance, nature con-servation and lack of staff/wardens. On the whole, women gave higher ratings than men to the environmental aspects of parks but were more critical about the provision and condition of certain facilities, particularly seats, toilets, shelter, staffing/policing and playgrounds.

There was a widespread perception in our research that the introduction of contract maintenance and mobile park wardens in place of traditional park keepers has contributed to a decline in maintenance standards and more anti-social behaviour in parks. This in turn has led to anxiety on the part of a significant minority of users, particularly women, about safety and the

appropriate use of parks. This conflict between activities and between
different users was a recurrent theme in comments made by visitors,
particularly in the Islington survey. This may have been exacerbated by the
small size of the parks and the limited resources of the Council compared with
the Royal Parks Agency. Some of these themes were echoed in the reasons
given by respondents to the Islington household survey for not visiting parks.
Overall, 37% of people in Islington visit parks regularly or occasionally. Whilst
this is a high figure relative to other leisure facilities, there is a large latent
demand which is frustrated by personal constraints such as the care of
children or elderly relatives or no access to a car, or by perceptual barriers
such as safety or a belief that the parks are poorly cared for.

One of the major factors said to influence women's perception and use of
urban parks is that of personal safety. This has been highlighted by several
studies such as Burgess *et al.* (1988) and Comedia (1995). The Royal Parks
study revealed that a small but significant proportion of women felt unsafe in
the park (5% compared with 3% of men). Safety, however, is a complex issue
and it should be noted that perception and behaviour may not be directly
related. For men, concerns were found to be mainly about the danger posed
by cyclists or cars in the park travelling too fast, whereas for women, the
reasons were often about feelings of vulnerability to attack in remote,
secluded or quiet areas, and the lack of wardens or park police, and
inadequate lighting. The nuisance caused by dogs was also a worry to many
women. Some of these anxieties may have been child related. These concerns
were also manifest in some of the improvements suggested by women such as
a greater security presence. Concerns about safety were more pronounced in
the Islington study. Here 12% of women reported feeling unsafe (compared
with 4% of men). Many of these, somewhat surprisingly, were young women
below 25 which contrasts with other research such as Scraton and Watson
(1998). Frequent visitors tended to feel more unsafe than other groups,
perhaps because they were often using the parks at either end of the day.
Many of those who reported feeling unsafe felt the lighting was poor and/or
there was insufficient staff.

Other interesting findings from the Islington survey related to the
response of visitors to questions on whether or not alcohol, begging, busking,
or music should be allowed in parks. Women in particular were strongly
against alcohol (67% cf 57% of men), and begging (80% cf 76%), but were less
concerned about busking and were slightly in favour overall of music in the
parks. The results show quite clearly that there are strong views about the
appropriateness of certain activities in the parks. This appears to be based on
safety fears or social attitudes generally, rather than resistance to forms of
leisure which may disturb the quiet environment of the park. This was

corroborated by evidence from the survey that a majority of women were in favour of more events and activities in the park.

Of course, a visitor survey is not necessarily the most appropriate vehicle for investigating safety issues. Evidence from the Islington household survey, however, confirmed that fears about safety does inhibit use of parks. In this survey 53% of women (compared with 39% of men) said improving security would encourage them to visit more often, whilst 46% of women (34% of men) would visit more often if lighting was improved. Whilst many park authorities are now beginning to address the issue of safety in parks, by introducing security measures, some respondents in our surveys felt that this would be too intrusive and insensitive in what should be a natural environment. Other authors (e.g. Comedia) have also suggested that overt security may have the effect of heightening existing tensions and that the most effective way to alleviate concerns about safety is to increase the use of parks through improvements to the infrastructure and staffing, through a greater number and variety of activities, and through greater community involvement. Our research tends to support these views since the Royal Parks, which are high quality, well used facilities with the active involvement of Friends groups, exhibit fewer social and perceptual problems than the parks in Islington which do not share these advantages.

One of the characteristics of women's use of parks compared with that of men is the fluctuation throughout their life course. This is usually associated with the presence of children or grandchildren or of other care responsibilities or particular friendships. In the Islington household survey, 19% of women reported that they visited local parks more than they used to and 39% reported that they used them less. In many cases the reasons for using parks less were connected with the stage of life but negative attitudes towards parks was also a significant factor. These results, which were to a lesser extent mirrored by the response from men, seem to confirm the general perception that use of urban parks is declining, and is in contrast with trends for most other leisure activities. It is also at variance with research which shows that people are taking an increased interest in the natural environment and ecology.

Other results from our research show that, on the whole, the reasons why women don't use parks are not because of a lack of interest or ability, but because their local parks don't offer the kind of activities or experience available in parks elsewhere. This is due either to the small size of the parks, their urban character, their lack of facilities or activities or their quality of maintenance. Only 20% of women appear to lack interest in parks, and a further 9% are concerned about the possible danger.

Interestingly, a majority of the suggestions for improvements made by both visitors and respondents to the household survey came from women, and these indicate where resources should be directed to achieve a greater level and equality of visitor use and satisfaction. Suggestions obviously varied from one park to another but there was general agreement on the need for more shelter, more staff, more lighting, more seats, less dog mess, better toilet facilities, more flowers, more signs and publicity and more or improved refreshments. More creative suggestions included fountains, sculpture and outdoor theatre. The promotion of a wider range of events and activities also featured highly in women's responses.

Conclusion

The Royal Parks and the parks within the Borough of Islington have differing roles, characteristics and management structures and stimulate numerous responses from visitors. However, there are similarities in terms of the visitor characteristics, patterns of use and perceptions of the park environments. Both studies support previous claims that women's leisure is constrained differently to men's and demonstrate how structural and inter-personal constraints are particularly influential in this respect. Urban parks themselves have been developed as social spaces and have evolved as land-scapes which communicate cultural messages. For example, the Victorian values of decency and propriety associated with parks (Cosgrove in Gregory and Walford, 1989) suggest that there are socially acceptable and deviant forms of behaviour which are different for men and women and the land-scapes themselves play a part in maintaining patriarchal dominance. This is illustrated in the behavioural and attitudinal differences between men and women highlighted in the research. Thus urban parks should be viewed as gendered landscapes which produce differing emotional responses. For many people parks evoke topophilia and thereby can be seen as valuable resources but for some people, particularly women, they are landscapes of fear and elicit topophobia. Policy, planning and management strategies should recognise these socio-cultural dimensions and their implications.

Both London parks studies have shown high percentages of commuter use (either travel to work or in lunchtimes) which could be one of the main causes of the male dominance of usage figures which contrast with previous research. Both studies show, through the high usage figures and apparent latent demand, that parks are socially important landscapes for leisure compared to other public facilities and that they are often more important as leisure venues for women than for men. This is emphasised by the more local nature of park usage by women and the socially oriented purpose of women's visits. For example, women are less likely to have access to a car, therefore rely on walking and public transport which may be influential in the use of more local facilities. This suggests, therefore, that from a woman's perspective more emphasis should be placed on provision of small local parks than larger more distant parks. This is relevant to the current open spaces planning study being carried out by CELTS for the London Planning Advisory Committee (LPAC) and could be achieved through redressing the balance of resource allocation between those parks deemed to be of regional significance and those which provide a vital service for local communities.

Notwithstanding methodological difficulties with measuring satisfaction, generally visitors appeared to be satisfied with the parks. The Royal Parks evoked higher levels of satisfaction which is not surprising given their history of dedicated and specialist management and higher funding levels compared to the limited resources available to maintain and develop the Islington parks. Men and women identified similar problems but women were more critical of facilities such as seats, toilets, shelter, staffing/policing and playgrounds, which demonstrates the importance of security measures and women's role as carers.

It could be argued that women tending to visit in social groups or accompanied by children is a product of their role as carers, visiting local facilities but it is also likely that the presence of others (friends, children, elderly relatives or dogs) provide a sense of security to the women. This offers some support for Valentine's (1989: p. 387) claim that "as a product of their fear, many women not only perceive, but also experience, their environment differently to men". Thus, in addition to having limited lifeworlds (Simmons, 1993) in spatial terms, the women may have adapted their behaviour and constrained their experience of the park landscape because of their fear, thereby further constraining their lifeworlds.

As gendered landscapes, parks are perceived and used differently by men and women with women possibly seeing themselves as, and exhibiting the constrained behaviour of, the 'other'. Therefore it is important that park authorities address the issue of providing for those who may be perceived, by themselves or others, as the 'other'. Obviously policy makers and managers can only begin to address some of the practical aspects which play a role in the cultural construction of place and women's perceptions of parks. For example, Valentine (1992) points out that the factors influencing perceptions of fear are predominantly structural.

Cloke and Little (1997: p. 279) also suggest that the cultural construction of identities of places are "rooted in a set of assumptions, expectations and values ... [which] ... rest on (and in turn reinforce) largely unchallenged meanings and beliefs". However, they also suggest that these are not fixed so it is imperative that parks initiate programmes to play an active role in changing the identity of parks. The London parks research has identified some specific management implications although it is recognised that such practical measures will have little impact on the effect of the patriarchal society, the current (infra) structure of the urban environment and its effect on women's lives and may be criticised (e.g. Greed, 1994; McDowell and Sharp, 1997) for addressing the symptom rather than the cause of gender difference. There is also a need for more structural changes broadly and specifically. For example, in terms of planning, Greed (1996b) suggests that more women need to be involved in policy making and planning processes, as professionals and in consultation exercises, if urban areas are to be accessible and viable places for women. This is also true in terms of parks but it is believed that if existing parks work towards providing an environment in which women feel a sense of belonging, ownership and security perhaps more women will visit the parks and use them with more freedom. This would in turn help to provide a more women-friendly environment for further broadening of appeal.

Physical barriers and travel to the parks have been identified as problems for women. This is rooted in the fact that most of the parks were provided prior to the major rise in car ownership and suburban expansion of towns and cities. Therefore contemporary, segmented urban forms do not lend themselves to ease of access to inner city parks. This is particularly true for women for whom travel on public transport is difficult such as the elderly, disabled and those travelling with young children. Crossing busy roads, using buses and negotiating the many staircases in the tube system are examples of the problems created by an urban form which has an economic basis, illustrating that the needs of those outside the economy are rarely considered (Rose, 1993). It is also of note that very few women cycled to the parks. Whilst this points to a general problem of cycling in urban areas, park authorities can help by providing better and safer cycle parks.

The London parks research has shown that despite the fact that parks are often visited for their peaceful properties, women feel more secure in areas which are used by other people rather than remote landscapes. Therefore, there is a need to improve the usage of the parks without causing over crowding and recognising that not everyone will be interested in park visiting. This may take the form of redistributing visitor patterns spatially or temporally as well as promoting an aggregate increase in usage. This is not an easy task but with further research and careful management, peopling the parks could be achieved. The London parks need to raise awareness of their assets and activities in order to promote an open door to those not currently utilising them. Managed sensitively this could promote usage by various groups of 'others' including women. One approach to developing the social dimension of parks valued by women is to develop community use through planning a varied programme of events and activities. For example, Regents Park stages a series of summer events, many of which are rather traditional, but some aim to attract under-represented groups including children and young people. Community oriented or community run programmes could equally be run at a more local level which could generate a greater sense of ownership. It may also help to provide some more positive common experiences and social contact (Valentine, 1992), thus providing opportunities for media coverage of the inclusive nature of these leisure facilities. Other initiatives may include self help groups such as women's walking networks (Jones and Crowe, 1995). An example of this is the Milton Keynes Women's Walking Network which stemmed from a parks survey which was followed up with women's focus groups based around organised walks. From this has developed an annual programme of walks for women. Such grass roots projects are not to the exclusion of tourism and other income generating activities. On the contrary, Wearing and Wearing (1996: p. 50) believe that, "rather than the image and the fleeting tourism gaze, the genuine social fabric may provide a more enduring tourist attraction" thereby allowing the parks to play a role in the image creation and place boosting increasingly expected from public leisure facilities.

Despite the fact that overall men are more likely than women to suffer personal attack (Valentine, 1992), a significant minority of women perceive parks as landscapes of fear and hence either avoid entering them, only visit at certain times with other people or restrict their spatial behaviour within them. Therefore it is imperative that this issue is given serious consideration. Security in the form of staffing rather than policing was an important issue for the women involved in the London parks research, particularly in Islington, as in other projects (Smyth and Pearlman, 1995; Burgess *et al.*, 1988). Therefore further consideration needs to be given to the visibility of staff currently employed in parks but also more investigation into the demands of women in this respect is necessary. For example, Burgess *et al.* (1988) suggest that a reduction in staff has reduced access for the more vulnerable but Ravenscroft (1995) and Comedia (1995) suggest that over-policing may increase anxiety levels and therefore be counter-productive. It is important that any such staffing or policing is unobtrusive and doesn't detract from the sense of getting away from it (and them) all that many respondents enjoy.

Practical infra-structural developments to improve personal security which were suggested in our research included improved lighting, which supports Nelson's (1997) findings on car parks. Cutting back vegetation was also felt to be a desirable landscape alteration in order to reduce hiding places for potential attackers. However, this would have amenity impacts thereby the effectiveness would need to be balanced with the resulting landscape change.

The provision of information was also perceived to be a weakness of current provision which may be a contributory factor in the creation of fear.

For example, when entering an unfamiliar or unknown environment, objective information about the spatial structure helps to reassure. This may also be related to a desire for (knowledge of) more exit points from the parks as indicated in the Islington research. Interpretation on the other hand can help to demonstrate how the social history of an environment may be relevant to the visitor in contemporary society and assist with visitor management (Glyptis, 1991). In this respect interpretation has the potential to provide a welcome for those previously being viewed as outsiders. Previous research has argued that the environmental quality of urban parks is declining. Overall, our research has shown that users are satisfied with them, although satisfaction levels in the Islington parks were considerably less. This is rather an unfair comparison since the Royal Parks are exceptional in their funding and management structures and therefore are not typical, although they offer a possible model of good practice. Islington's parks provide an example of the theory that parks, in common with other forms of social provision, reflect the environment in which they are located. For example, it may be claimed that the parks should be improved as a catalyst for environmental improvements and care for the environment by local residents and visitors. Alternatively, it could be argued that unless the surrounding area is improved (e.g. graffiti and litter removed) then the parks will be fighting a losing battle. A park visit, in common with some other types of leisure activities, is a composite product in which travel to the park, as a component of the overall experience, plays a major role. In the London parks research, women tended to be more environmentally aware and concerned therefore it appears to be important to provide a well maintained environment both within and outside the park if women are to perceive the park to be a desirable landscape rather than provoking feelings of topophobia.

Clearly, these findings raise questions about the research techniques used. These range from methodological questions about respondent selection, response rates and questionnaire design to more philosophical issues about the positivist nature of the studies. The positivist paradigm within which the studies were conducted was determined by the objectives of the studies which in turn were largely influenced by the clients. This is one of the constraints in undertaking client based research. Whilst quality controls were rigorously applied in the survey design and implementation process, the lack of a more qualitative approach to triangulate the research was a weakness. This is perhaps especially so when trying to measure visitor satisfaction, although many studies (e.g. Ryan, 1995) have used attitudinal scales in the way in which we did to address this psychological issue. One of the advantages of our approach was that a very large sample was obtained and the results can therefore be validated statistically. This is important when dealing with questions of performance measurement and when arguing for policy, funding and management changes.

The Royal Parks and Islington Borough parks research has shown that women perceive and use parks differently to men and thus may be viewed as marginalised in what are ostensibly facilities provided for all to access equally. Thus some operational suggestions have been given for implementing solutions to some of the perceived barriers, encouraging more women to use the parks with a sense of personal security. However, the suggestions have resource implications and thus would require further investigation, sensitive management and ongoing evaluation to ensure effectiveness. Such pragmatic considerations can only play a small part in any process of emancipating women in terms of their use of the urban leisure environment, so it is vital that parks as significant amenities, particularly for women, are recognised as part of the political and social agenda.

References

Aitken, S. C. and Rushton, G. (1993) 'Perceptual and behavioural theory in practice', *Progress in Human Geography* Vol. 17, No. 3: pp. 378–388.

Appleton, J. (1996) *The experience of landscape* (Revised edition) Chichester: Wiley.

Bale, J. (1989) *Sports geography*. London: Spon.

——— (1992) *Sport, space and the city*. London: Routledge.

Bondi, L. (1992) 'Gender symbols and urban landscapes', *Progress in Human Geograpy* Vol. 16, No. 2: pp. 157–170.

Burgess, J. (1996) 'Focusing on fear: The use of focus groups in a project for the Community Forest Unit, Countryside Commission', *Area*, Vol. 28, No. 2: pp. 130–135.

Burgess, J., Harrison, C. M. and Limb, M. (1988) 'People, parks and the urban green: A study of popular meanings and values for open spaces in the city', *Urban Studies* 25: pp. 455–473.

Cloke, P. and Little, J. (1997) *Contested countryside cultures; Otherness, marginalisation and rurality*. London: Routledge.

Comedia (1995) *Parklife: Urban parks and social renewal*. Stroud: Comedia.

Cosgrove, D. and Daniels, S. (eds) (1988) *The iconography of landscape*. Cambridge: Cambridge University Press.

Curson, T. (1995a) 'Can you place your trust in them ? The role of charitable trusts in leisure management', in D. Leslie (ed) _Tourism and leisure — perspectives on provision._ LSA Publication No. 52. Eastbourne: Leisure Studies Association, pp. 63–79.

—— (1995b) _People using the Royal Parks: Annual Report 1994._ London: CELTS / UNL Press.

—— (1996) _People using the Royal Parks: Annual Report 1995._ London: CELTS / UNL Press.

—— (1997) _Islington Parks: Report of visitor and household surveys._ CELTS for London Borough of Islington.

Deem, R. (1986) _All work and no play? A study of women and leisure._ Milton Keynes: Open University Press.

Duncan, N. (ed) (1996) _BodySpace._ London: Routledge.

Evans, G. (1997) _Trends in outdoor pursuits._ London: CELTS for the Health Education Authority, University of North London.

Eyles, J. (1985) _Senses of place._ Warrington: Silverbrook Press.

Glyptis, S. (1991) _Countryside recreation._ Harlow: Longman / ILAM.

Greed, C. (1994) _Women and planning: Creating gendered realities._ London: Routledge.

Greed, C. (1996a) 'Planning for women and other disenabled groups, with reference to the provision of public toilets in Britain', _Environment and Planning_ A, 28: pp. 573–588.

Greed, C. (1996b) _Introducing town planning._ (2nd ed) Harlow: Longman.

Green, E. (1998) 'Women doing friendship: an analysis of women's leisure as a site of identity construction, empowerment and resistance', _Leisure Studies_, Vol. 17, pp. 171–185.

Green, E., Hebron, S. and Woodward, D. (1987) _Leisure and gender — a study of Sheffield women's leisure experiences._ London: Sports Council and ESRC.

Gregory, D. and Walford, R (1989) _Horizons in human geography._ London: Macmillan.

Hargreaves, J. (1994) _Sporting females: Critical issues in the history and sociology of women's sports._ London: Routledge.

Henderson, K.A., Bialeschki, M. D., Shaw, S. M. and Freysinger V. J. (1996) _Both gains and gaps: Feminist perspectives on women's leisure._ State College, PA.: Venture Publishing.

Jackson, P. (1989) _Maps of meaning._ London: Routledge.

Jencks, C. A. (1978) *The language of postmodern architecture*. London: Academy Editions.

Jones, M. and Crowe, L. (1995) Unpublished paper, 'Unequal opportunities ? The continued problem of lack of universal access by urban populations to informal recreation in the urban fringe', Recreation in the City conference.

Keith, M. and Pile, S. (eds) (1993) *Place and the politics of identity*. London: Routledge.

Lewin, K. (1936) *Principles of topological psychology*. New York: Mcgraw-Hill.

London Boroughs Association (1995) *Watch this space*. London: London Boroughs Association.

London Planning Advisory Committee (1988) *Strategic planning advice for London*. London: LPAC.

Marshall, N. and Wood, P. (1995) *Services and space: Key aspects of urban and regional development*. Harlow: Longman.

Massey, D. (1984) *Spatial divisions of labour: Social structures and the geography of production*. Basingstoke: Macmillan.

———— (1993) 'Politics and space/time', in M. Keith and S. Pile (eds) *Place and the politics of identity*. London: Routledge.

MATRIX (1984) *Making space*. London: Pluto Press.

McDowell, L. (1990) 'Gender matters: Feminism / postmodernism in Glasgow and Toronto', *Area* 22: pp. 387–390.

McDowell, L. and Sharp, J. P. (eds) (1997) *Space, gender, knowledge: Feminist readings*. London: Wiley.

Milton Keynes Development Corporation (1988) *Study of the use and perception of parks in Milton Keynes 1988*. Recreation Unit Study 18. Milton Keynes: Milton Keynes Development Corporation .

Milton Keynes Parks Trust (1995a) *Report on parks visitor surveys 1995*. Milton Keynes: Milton Keynes Parks Trust.

Milton Keynes Parks Trust (1995b) *Attitudes towards and and perceptions of parks in Milton Keynes*. Milton Keynes: Milton Keynes Parks Trust.

Mowl, G. and Towner, J. (1995) 'Women, gender, leisure and place: Towards a more "humanistic" geography of women's leisure', *Leisure Studies* Vol. 14: pp. 102–116.

Nelson, A. (1997) 'Fear of parking', *Town and Country Planning* (January): p. 3.

OPCS (1993) *General Household Survey*. London: HMSO.

Page, S., Nielson, K. and Goodenough, R. (1994) 'Managing urban parks: User perspectives and local leisure needs in the 1980s', *Service Industries Journal*, Vol. 14, No. 2.

Pain, R. (1991) 'Space, sexual violence and social control: integrating geographical and feminist analyses of women's fear of crime', *Progress in Human Geography* Vol. 15, No. 4: 415–431.

—— (1997) 'Social geographies of women's fear of crime', *Transactions of Institute of British Geographers*, 22: pp. 231–244.

Penning-Rowsell, E. (1982) 'Public preference of landscape quality', *Regional Studies* 16: pp. 97–112.

Pocock, D. (1993) 'The senses in focus', *Area* Vol. 25, No. 1: pp. 11–16.

Rapoport, A. (1982) *The meaning of the built environment*. London:Sage

Ravenscroft, N. (1995) 'Expectation versus provision in the management and use of urban open space', Unpublished paper, Recreation in the City Conference.

Relph, E. (1976) *Place and placelessness*. London: Pion.

Richards, G. and Curson, T. (1993) *Market research methodology study for the Royal Parks*. London: CELTS, University of North London.

Rose, G. (1993) *Feminism and geography: The limits of geographical knowledge*. London: Pion.

Ryan, C. (1995) *Researching tourist satisfaction*. London: Routledge.

Sayers, P. (1993) *Managing sport and leisure facilities: A guide to competitive tendering*. London: Spon.

Scraton, S. and Watson, B. (1998) 'Gendered cities: women and public leisure space in the "postmodern city"', *Leisure Studies* Vol.17: pp. 123-137.

Simmons, I. G. (1993) *Interpreting nature: Cultural construction of the environment*. London: Routledge.

Sharma, P. (1993) *Opening the door a bit wider*. Newham Leisure Services.

Smyth, K and Pearlman, D. (1995) 'Open spaces — closed places ? A small scale study of the use of urban parks by ethnic minority groups in the London Borough of Newham', Unpublished paper, Recreation in the City conference.

Tuan, Y-F (1974) *Topophilia*. Englewood Cliffs, NJ: Prentice-Hall.

—— (1977) *Space and place: The perspective of experience*. London: Arnold.

Urry, J. (1990) *The tourist gaze*. London: Sage.

—— (1995) *Consuming places*. London: Routledge.

Valentine, G. (1989) 'The geography of women's fear', *Area* Vol. 21, No. 4: pp. 385–390.

—— (1992) 'Images of danger: Women's sources of information about the spatial distribution of male violence', *Area* Vol. 24, No. 1: pp. 22–29.

Walker, S. E. and Duffield, B. S. (1983) *Urban parks and open spaces — A review*. Edinburgh: Tourism and Recreation Research Unit, University of Edinburgh.

Walmsley, D. J. and Lewis, G. J. (1993) *People and environment: Behavioural approaches in human geography*. Harlow: Longman.

Wearing, B. and Wearing, S. (1996) 'Phallic fallacy in accessing leisure spaces', *Environment Paper Series*, pp. 37–53.

Wimbush, E. (1986) *Women, leisure and well-being*. Edinburgh: Centre for Leisure Research.

Wimbush, E. and Talbot, M. (eds) (1988) *Relative freedoms — Women and leisure*. Milton Keynes: Open University Press.

Williams, S. (1995) *Outdoor recreation and the urban environment*. London: Routledge.

Williams, S. and Jackson, G. A. M. (1985) 'Recreational use of public open space in the Potteries conurbation', *Occasional Papers in Geography*, No 15. Stoke on Trent: Staffordshire Polytechnic.

Wilson, E. (1991) *The sphinx in the city: Urban life, the control of disorder and women*. London: Virago Press.

Women's Design Service (1993) *Planning London: Unitary development plans*. London: WDS.

Recognising Women: Discourses in Outdoor Education

Di Collins

Buckinghamshire Chilterns University College

Introduction

> Women were noticeably in the minority at the international gatherings which formulated conceptions of environmental education. The absence of women can be seen as being related to the epistemological framework of environmental education being very much that of a man-made subject and to the content of the corresponding curriculum and research programmes tending to be determined by male agenda. (Gough, 1999: p. 143)

Annette Gough's comments could be equally applied to outdoor education. Both are relatively young areas of learning, having been formalised into their present positions in relation to formal and informal education in post war years. This paper reflects on going research into women's experiences of policy and practice in outdoor education. Here, I describe the gender bias of discourses on outdoor education, and discuss women in relation to outdoor education pedagogy and androgeny. Finally I offer a feminist poststructuralist perspective, which might enable currently silenced voices to be heard.

Outdoor education discourses

Over the past fifty years, outdoor education has been evolving. It has developed from the field of outdoor activity and character building, largely based on Kurt Hahn's insights (Richardson, 1990) to using the many attributes of the outdoors for personal, group and organisational development, for

29

supporting reflection on the forces that have shaped the environment and the self. This might be summarised as follows:

> Outdoor education is an experiential method of learning with the use of all senses. It takes place primarily, but not exclusively, through exposure to the natural environment. In outdoor education, the emphasis for the subject of learning is placed on relationships concerning people and natural resources. (Priest, 1990: p. 113)

However, just as outdoor pursuits were predominantly regarded as the right of European and North American men "to test their strength, develop self-confidence, and achieve dominance" (Fox, 1997: p. 161) and as the implied connection between humans and the environment in outdoor activity has been diminished, so outdoor education was seen as the haunt for young men. Initially young women were excluded from Outward Bound courses and expeditioning in the Duke of Edinburgh's Award Scheme.

Therefore, with this background, it is hardly surprising that models for outdoor education practice are dominated by male writers. In the 1970s and 1980s, these writers described holistic, integrative processes, and the relationship with the environment and the impact of peak experiences within these, using approaches such as "letting the experience speak for itself", speaking for the experience and debriefing the experience. (e.g. Cornell, 1979; Mortlock, 1984; Van Matre 1972). However, in more recent years, there has been a move toward more structured learning, as the potential of outdoor education for adventure or wilderness therapy, corporate learning, or team building has been recognised. Gass (1995: pp. 1–2) writes of a gradual evolution in the facilitating of adventure experiences away from those holistic processes to more sophisticated approaches, such as directly 'frontloading'[1] the experience, framing the experience and indirectly frontloading the experiences. He suggests a philosophical shift between the two groups of reviewing processes, based "on the use of proactive techniques to ... enhance a client's adventure experience and its future applications" (1995: p. 2).

In these latter situations, the outdoor environment has become a class-room setting for achieving particular outcomes, rather than an integral component of a total experience. Any celebration of the characteristics of a particular environment may be incidental. Thus, aspects of the definition which refer to the environment may be overlooked (Webb 1997: p. 394). Heidi Mack has also criticised these proactive, sophisticated review processes, described by Gass (1995: pp. 1–2), as symptomatic of a 'male' model of facilitating learning.

Their emphasis on standardised outcomes lend themselves to manipulation of power and process. Mack describes them as "the imposed metaphor model":

> ... not only must the instructor assess the client's needs, provide a safe physical environment, and ensure the transfer of learning to real-life settings, but she/he 'must also provide appropriate forming and structuring of the experience for the client' (Gass, 1993: 226). This means an application of what might be considered a heavy and paternalistic hand in creating and directing the metaphoric activity. (1996: p. 24)

Women's voices have been largely invisible in the development and recording of these outdoor education strategies and processes. There are a few exceptions. For example, Barbara Humberstone (e.g. 1990, 1996, 1998) has written widely about gender bias in the United Kingdom. In North America, a number of writers have promoted women's perspectives. For example, Karen Warren (1996) has helped to rectify the imbalance by incorporating the work of a number of women outdoor educators in *Women's Voices in Experiential Education*. There are also growing numbers of publications on ecofeminism. However, these and other works are swamped by the materials generated by men. Moreover (perhaps surprisingly), for some practitioners women in leadership roles still require legitimisation. For example, Graham felt the need to include a chapter dispelling myths about women leaders. In his book on outdoor leadership, he writes:

> Many men are quite comfortable with this growing trend (of women leaders), but some are not... It's this resentment that is the catalyst for much of the petty biases and double standards that deplore women. (1997: pp. 41–42).

Women have also been marginalised at many international gatherings focussing on outdoor education. At the 1996 European Congress, 'Youth and Social Work on the Move: Second conference on youth and social work through adventure and the outdoors', a special plea had to be made for workshops focusing on the needs of young women. This imbalance was largely rectified at the third congress, 'Learning by Sharing Cultural Differences'. However, the European Institute on Outdoor Adventure Education and Experiential Learning's board has eight members. One is a woman. When women's voices are heard, they tend to be those of white European, North American or Australasian English-speakers.

The experience and voices of black women are further marginalised. Bachendri Pal focuses her work on young women because:

> I feel that in India we neglect them [young women] and discourage them from outdoor pursuits. (1992: p. 137)

Her contributions to the knowledge about women, the outdoors and nature are not being heard. Where voices are being heard, patronising attitudes continue to exist. Vandana Shiva's (1998) work has had an impact on understandings of women's relationship with nature and environment. However, she demurs the pursuance of the supremacy of Western thinking in a postcolonial age. Moreover, the beliefs of other women may be taken out of context. Noel Sturgeon describes the violation of North American Indian spirituality, through its inappropriate application (1997: 270). On a positive note, Judy Ling Wong (1998) describes the linking of ethnic identity with environmental identity as a means of integration rather than subjugation into new ways of life.

Women and outdoor education: andragogy and pedagogy

The lack of research into how young women and women learn through outdoor education limits understandings and analyses of its mechanisms and potential. Jarvis *et al.* (1998: p. 68) acknowledge that models of adult learning and definitions of adulthood are based on sexist assumptions. They suggest that research has done little to explore whether there is anything special or different in the ways in which women learn. Similar criticisms may be made of children's learning, although there have been studies into gender and outdoor education (Humberstone, 1986) and it is known that young women are less likely to opt for an outdoor education experience than young men (Mason 1995).

   Gilligan's work (1982) explains that women define themselves and their knowledge in terms of their relationships and that women's selves are formed through learning in social, and generally informal, contexts. Thus a formal outdoor education environment might have limitations for women's learning. Attitudes to and understandings of the outdoors are also critical. However, women's ways of knowing are influenced by the impact of male power. Whilst postmodernism has supported and celebrated the 'deconstruction' and even fragmentation of meanings of such social constructions as 'environment' and 'nature' (Barry, 1999: pp. 166–167), these 'knowings' may be a response to or an adaptation of women's experiences, and may not fully take conscious account of male forces. Thus, it may be male 'ownership' of 'human-created' or 'culture' that leaves 'environment 'or 'nature' more accessible to women and the technology and skills associated with outdoor education more accessible to men (Mellor, 1997: pp. 125–126).

Wearing (1998: p. 149) suggests that, in general, women and men have different understandings of leisure, the context in which outdoor education might occur. Women may regard leisure as "personal spaces, physical and metaphorical, where women can explore their own desires and pleasures and perform acts which allow them to become women in their own right, to constitute diverse subjectivities and femininities which go beyond what women have been told they should be." Furthermore, she points to theories that suggest that, for many men, leisure is the necessary process for the proving of masculinity and the reconstructing of masculinities that are not the same as women's subjectivities (Wearing. 1998: pp. 83–84).

Outdoor education from a feminist poststructuralist perspective

Feminist postructuralist perspectives have key roles to play in supporting outdoor education's 'coming of age' and its transformation from the bounded field of outdoor education to the open 'moorland' of outdoor learning. (Usher *et al.*, 1997: p. 26) Implicit in this is the recognition that subjectivity, the 'knowings' and 'beings' are not fixed or universal, but constantly in process, being constituted and reconstituted, partial, multiple and contradictory and located within the social context from which they originate. This can lead to an acceptance that there is no 'one way'. This broadening of understanding can be advanced by listening to the marginalised:

> We should be looking at texts for who is saying what and for what purpose, looking for the gaps and silences in those texts, and asking questions about whether the discourses are of interest to us to start from others' lives or perpetuate the dominant discourses. (Gough, 1999: p. 158)

This emancipatory research involves taking note of the Western, English-speaking domination of the published word in outdoor education; starting research from the perspectives of those who have been silenced, appreciating and understanding these women's stories; recognising that the knowledge of some women is no less significant for being anecdotal (Curtin, 1997: p. 87); and giving voice to the research participants in order to empower. Texts in other areas of learning can be studied to help identify gaps and find possible solutions. For example, feminist geographers have described the need to challenge the accepted conventions of academic writing.

... creating a space of resistance, a space from which to challenge the hierarchies, assumptions, language and conventions of the male-dominated world ... (Rose *et al.*, 1997: p. 3)

This celebration of the wealth and diversity of 'knowings' in relation to outdoor education can be instrumental in promoting the paradigm shift to outdoor learning.

Conclusion

The male-dominated, English-speaking interpretations of outdoor education have been questioned in the light of the experience of white women, Black and Asian women and non-English speaking women. However, it is recognised that diverse groups of women have a significant role to play in enabling outdoor education to develop beyond its present constraints. This involves placing the learner, the woman, in a central position. The diversity and flexibility of outdoor education is potentially its strength.

Note

[1] Frontloading — developing an experience in order to bring about certain outcomes.

References

Barry, J. (1999) *Environment and social theory*. London: Routledge.

Cornell, J.B. (1979) *Sharing nature with children*. Watford, Herts.: Exley Publications.

Curtin, D. (1997) 'Women's knowledge as expert knowledge: Indian women and ecodevelopment', in K.J. Warren (ed) *Ecofeminism: Women, culture, vature*. Bloomington: Indiana University Press.

Fox, K.M. (1997) 'Leisure: Celebration and resistance in the ecofeminist quilt', in K.J. Warren (ed) *Ecofeminism: Women, culture, nature*. Bloomington: Indiana University Press.

Gass, M.A. (1993) *Adventure therapy: Therapeutic applications of adventure programming*. Dubuque, Iowa: Kendall/Hunt Publishing.

Gass, M. A. (1995) *Book of metaphors*. Dubuque, IA: Kendall/ Hunt.

Gilligan, C. (1982) *In a different voice: Psychological theory and women's development*. Cambridge, Mass.: Harvard University Press.

Gough, A. (1999) 'Recognising women in environmental education pedagogy and research: Toward an ecofeminist poststructuralist perspective', *Environmental Education Research* Vol. 5, No.2: pp. 143–162.

Graham, J. (1997) *Outdoor leadership: Technique, common sense and self-confidence*. Seattle, WA: The Mountaineers.

Humberstone, B. (1986) 'A study of gender and schooling in outdoor education', in J. Evans (ed) *Physical education, sport and schooling: Studies in the sociology of physical education*. London: Falmer Press.

Humberstone, B. (1990) 'Gender, change and adventure education', *Gender and Education*. Vol.2, No.2: pp. 215–231.

Humberstone, B. (1996) 'Other voices: Many meanings? Women and the outdoors', *Journal of Adventure Education and Outdoor Leadership* Vol. 13, No. 2: pp. 40–46.

Humberstone, B. (1998) 'Re-creation and connection in and with nature: Synthesising ecological and feminist discourses', *The International Review for the Sociology of Sport* Vol. 33, No.4: pp. 367–380.

Luckner, J. L. and Nadler, R. S. (1997) (2nd ed) *Processing the experience: Strategies to enhance and generalize learning*. Dubuque, IA: Kendall/ Hunt.

Jarvis, P., Holford, J. and Griffin, C. (1998) *The theory and practice of learning*. London: Kogan Page.

Mack, H. (1996) 'Inside work, outdoors: Women, metaphor, and meaning', in K. Warren (ed) (1996) *Women's voices in experiential education*. Dubuque, Iowa: Kendall/Hunt Publishing.

Mason, V. (1995) *Sport in England*. London: Sports Council.

Mellor, M. (1997) *Feminism and ecology*. Cambridge: Polity Press.

Miles, J. and Priest, S. (eds.) (1990) *Adventure education*. State College, PA: Venture Publishing.

Mortlock, C. (1984) *The adventure alternative*. Cumbria: Cicerone Press.

Pal, Bachendri (1992) 'Everest: My journey to the top', in R. da Silva (ed) *Leading out: Women climbers reaching for the top*. Seattle, Washington: Seal Press.

Priest, S. (1990) 'The semantics of adventure education', in J. Miles and S. Priest (eds.) *Adventure education*. State College, PA: Venture Publishing.

Richardson, A. (1990) 'Kurt Hahn', in J. Miles and S. Priest (eds) *Adventure education*. State College, PA: Venture Publishing.

Rose, G., Gregson, N., Foord, J., Bowlby, S., Dywer, C., Holloway, S., Laurie, N., Maddrell, A. and Skelton, T. (1997) 'Introduction', in *Women and Geography Study Group Feminist Geographies: Explorations in diversity and difference.* Harlow: Longman.

Shiva, Vandana (1988) *Staying alive: Women, ecology and survival in India.* New Delhi: Kali for Women.

Sturgeon, N. (1997) 'The Nature of Race: Discourses of Racial Difference in Ecofeminism', in K.J. Warren, (ed) *Ecofeminism: Women, culture, nature.* Bloomington: Indiana University Press.

Usher, R., Bryant, I. and Johnston, R. (1997) *Adult education and the postmodern challenge: Learning beyond the limits.* London: Routledge.

Van Matre, S. (1972) *Acclimatization: A sensory and conceptual approach to ecological involvement.* Martinsville, IN.: American Camping Association.

Warren, K. (ed.) (1996) *Women's voices in experiential education.* Dubuque, Iowa: Kendall/Hunt Publishing.

Warren, K.J. (ed) (1997) *Ecofeminism: Women, culture, nature.* Bloomington: Indiana University Press.

Wearing, B. (1998) *Leisure and feminist theory.* London: Sage.

Webb, W. (1997) 'Spirituality: The spirit of nature', in J. L. Luckner and R. S. Nadler, (2nd ed.) *Processing the experience: Strategies to enhance and generalize learning.* Dubuque, IA: Kendall/ Hunt.

Women and Geography Study Group (1997) *Feminist geographies: Explorations in diversity and difference.* Harlow: Longman

Wong, Judy Ling (1998) 'Ethnic identity and integration in action', in P. Higgins and B. Humberstone (eds) *Cultural diversity: Learning by sharing cultural differences. Report of the Third European Congress for Outdoor Adventure Education and Experiential Learning.* Buckinghamshire Chilterns University College.

Gender Issues and Women's Windsurfing

Val Woodward

Department of Social Policy and Social Work, University of Plymouth, UK

My research

> By doing work where we have personal commitments, our academic contributions are more likely to come out of a personal, creative, politically engaged self, one that has a social — and not just academic — purpose. (Olsen, 1994: p. 201)

In 1994, as an enthusiastic windsurfer, committed political activist, unashamed feminist, and tentative academic, I started exploring the gendered experiences of women who windsurf. These explorations reflected my personal interest in how windsurfing made me feel. Primarily I loved the sensations of personal control, fresh air, physical movement and action. At first, I did not consciously register any of these as more frequently associated with masculinity than femininity (Allison, 1994; Mangan, 1995; Sabo and Runfola, 1980; Theberge, 1981), although I was aware that there were very few women windsurfing around me.

I had previously found myself in male dominated situations on varied and frequent occasions, most notably within party politics and I, along with other women, had struggled with the tensions between acting 'like a man' so as to be accepted, or acting 'differently' and being marginalised. Sometimes I chose to try to prove my competence using the criteria associated with the dominant discourses, at other times to press for changes as part of resisting those dominant discourses. Sometimes I felt I overcame barriers, but at other times I let them overcome me. When I later started to explore feminist writings in

37

some depth, I recognised these inconsistencies and struggles as ones associated with gender. By then I had begun to windsurf whenever I could, and
I noted the similarities in experience between my party political world and
that of my new leisure pursuit. Feminism helped me to understand my
complex feelings. I enjoyed the opportunities and challenges, but at the same
time I was often frustrated with myself and with others. I realised that the
apparently personal and intimate experiences buried within me could well be
familiar to others within my gender class. I therefore wanted to find out more
about the experiences of other women windsurfers, not just to help clarify
some of my own thoughts and feelings, but also to use our experiences to
further develop practical and theoretical understandings of gender through
the interpretation and conceptualisation of those experiences. I was not
looking for a truth, only a deeper comprehension of the complexities. This
personal approach is methodologically controversial as has been debated
extensively elsewhere. It is however one which informs and enhances this
study.

> Feminist theory seeks to analyse the conditions which shape women's
> lives and to explore cultural understandings of what it means to be a
> woman. (Jackson and Jones, 1998: p. 1)

Feminist interpretative perspectives reassess those interpretative frameworks
which reflect and perpetuate the dominant discourses. By taking a feminist
approach, the taken-for-granted characteristics of windsurfing can be
analysed so that gendered barriers can be identified and reconfigured. An
exploration of the experiences of women, who through their gender are not
part of the dominant discourse of windsurfing, offers us some different truths
which challenge the power of men to define the activity of windsurfing. It
seeks to alter the partial vision of reality which captures only the vision of the
powerful (Harding, 1991).

   I have collected qualitative data from women windsurfers at various
locations during the past few years and presented the findings to audiences
of both academics and windsurfers. Previous papers arising out of this
research have focused on gendered embodiment, sexuality and identity as
recognised by women who windsurf (Woodward, 1996; 1998; 1999). In this
paper the analysis moves towards policy recommendations arising out of
reflection on experiences gained through teaching windsurfing at women-only
sessions. As a windsurfing instructor I also have experience of teaching mixed
sex groups of adults and children and these are often male dominated. This
paper forms part of a continuous process of reflecting on and reassessing my

self identity as a windsurfing woman and my practice as a feminist windsurfing instructor.

My convictions led me to set up a women's windsurfing evening at a lake in Cornwall, utilising my learning about gender and windsurfing. As a participant observer I have been able to continue my previous work exploring the gendered experiences of windsurfing women through in-depth interviews and conversation. The words of women I have windsurfed with provide the evidence analysed within this paper. Quotations from them are interspersed throughout.

Women-only sessions

As a member of the organisation 'Windsurfing Women'[1], I am linked to a British network of women who aim to support women windsurfers through social and training events. 'WW', as it is usually referred to, is a loose knit voluntary organisation bringing together individuals with widely varying ideas as to what and why they organise under its umbrella. Some describe themselves as feminists. Others do not. WW, as an organisation, has not formally articulated what its supportive stance entails and this leaves women to interpret it for themselves. My own stance is an articulation derived from feminist theory, and also inspired by women I have met, observed, researched and had informal discussions with while windsurfing at different places within Britain and Europe including during some WW events.

Managers at the lake, where I work part-time as a windsurfing instructor, gave me a free hand as to what should happen at a women's session. The management of the facility is a complex one involving the owners of the lake and the windsurfing sporting body, the Royal Yachting Association, as well as the more direct involvement of staff employed at the centre. As with most sport and leisure bureaucracies there seems to be a hope that simply by providing more opportunities for participation for women, any constraints women may experience will be eliminated. However, the myriad of people involved in managing the lake, most of whom are male, showed a very varied commitment to considering the needs and purpose of sessions for women, some being very supportive and others dismissive or antagonistic.

> It is a central tenet of feminism that the achievement of so-called equality does not consist merely of being free to do whatever men have done, but first to question the moral and human consequences of the structures and procedures which have been created by patriarchal society to exclude women. Offering women's sessions does not in itself

deal with this exclusion. The equal right to be just like a man is not
the answer for someone who is actually a woman. (Chapman, 1993:
p. 161)

Feminist commentators have challenged approaches based on simply creating
more opportunities for women to participate in a male dominated activity,
instead suggesting that power inequalities have to be addressed (Goodale and
Witt, 1989; Humberstone, 1990; Scraton, 1986; Stanley, 1980; Talbot, 1988;
Vertinsky, 1992). Feminists have extensively theorised power so that women
can understand and resist facets of power which disadvantage women
through gender. Whilst empowerment as a concept is sometimes related to
individual advancement, here it is used as referring to a change in power
relations between groups or classes of men and women. At the weekly evening
sessions, I attempt to challenge some of the patriarchal power structures
which manifest themselves within windsurfing culture and to make
windsurfing empowering and more participant friendly for women both
through my organisation and teaching.

   Windsurfing is male dominated (Hornby, 1993) as is easily observable at
any windsurfing venue in Britain. Spare time, resources and freedom to
engage in pleasurable pursuits are a privilege in our unequal society and
associated with social groups enjoying the greatest wealth and power (Deem,
1986; Scraton, 1986; Wimbush and Talbot, 1988).

   Windsurfing is elitist because it involves having freedom, time and
   money. (Jessica)[2]

While I, and others, continue to stress the importance of keeping women's
sessions financially feasible for those with little personal financial freedom,
material inequalities do not seem to pose as large a barrier as freedom from
servicing others. Each week women phone to cancel because they have to look
after others. It is difficult to run classes as women tend to turn up at different
times, depending on when they can get away from their commitments.
Anything between eight and twenty women attend each week, with only two
consistently attending. They include women with a wide range of life stories,
skills and perspectives. The youngest is fourteen and the oldest in her early
fifties. They are not a representative sample of all women who windsurf, but
each is a woman who, consciously or not, pushes against the boundaries of
femininity. Their stories therefore provide interesting insights into gender
constructions and resistances as do the stories of other women I have met
windsurfing.

Women's evenings in Cornwall

Elitism not only manifests itself through lack of freedom, time and money, but also through competitive approaches to success and satisfaction. A male staff member at the lake, Paul, was completely bewildered when his description of windsurfing amongst large waves off the north coast of Cornwall, elicited the response from a women's night member:

> That's a completely different activity. (Angela)

To Angela, windsurfing in safe conditions on the lake each week is exciting, stimulating and satisfying. To Paul, windsurfing on the lake is practice for the 'real thing' when the windsurfer constantly fights waves and wind to show their daring, expertise and 'Go For It' attitude. One of the key elements in proving masculinity is the willingness to take risks (Allison, 1994; Mangan, 1995; Sabo and Runfola, 1980; Theberge, 1981). 'Go For It' is a phrase frequently heard amongst windsurfers:

> Men will go for things and women won't. It's the way they are brought up. Men aren't constantly having people warning them not to do things. (Linda)

Women who enjoy 'being one of the boys' tend to be ambivalent about the importance of safety:

> I have noticed that women seem to have more of a self preservation instinct. I don't know why it is and I know I'm quite reckless myself in lots of ways. (Pam)

Pam remembers how she was the only woman who windsurfed with a large group of men one day in Scotland. Nina and another woman had been part of the group earlier, but they went inland to a Loch once they assessed that the sea was too risky that day:

> That was the big difference... I thought if I go out, I could cope but I wouldn't enjoy it. I might break something but I might also just be wearing myself out for the sake of trying to survive in waves.... (Nina)

Later one of the men windsurfing out at sea had to be rescued. In the pub he recounted the story of his rescue proudly. He had been shown to have plenty of 'Go For It'. The two women who went to the Loch, on the other hand, would hate to need to be rescued:

> They put their lives at risk. They also put other people's lives at risk bringing the helicopter out. (Nina)

I have found that some men are wary of the 'dare-devil' attitude celebrated within dominant windsurfing culture and subsequently find it difficult to fully participate within that culture. The complexities of changing and varied masculinities within windsurfing are being explored (see Wheaton, 1998). We both acknowledge the valuable work being done more generally on sport and masculinity (e. g. Kimmel and Messner, 1993; Sabo and Gordon, 1995).

While the two women who went to the Loch would hate to need to be rescued they identified the presence or absence of rescue cover as an important factor to take into consideration when assessing where and when to windsurf:

> If I contrast myself and my husband, he seems to have greater confidence in his ability to get himself out of difficulties. (Jane)

A safe space is created on Tuesday evenings in Cornwall, which allows women to take some risks whilst exploring their abilities. The presence of a safety boat along with the site being an enclosed lake are reasons cited by women as to why they will happily windsurf at the lake, but are reluctant to go out on the sea with male friends:

> I think most women have got this fear that they can't do things and are therefore more safety conscious. (Ros)

When women first come to the sessions at lake, safety procedures are gone through in minute detail. I've heard so many women talk about the importance of safety:

> Maybe us allowing ourselves to worry so much is something to do with not having to prove ourselves as macho the way men feel they have to. (Lorraine)

Unlike boys and men, girls and women are not encouraged to be daring and push their limits (Crawford *et al.*, 1992). The male members of staff at the lake do not place such an emphasis on safety although they have to be safety conscious themselves as instructors. They think most people would find it restrictive and derogatory within the context of the dominant windsurfing culture.

Tuesday evening sessions emphasise the women's control, not just of their ability to get back to dry land, but also of their equipment. Simple things that are taken for granted the rest of the week are challenged. Participants in the sessions are not expected to carry the windsurfing boards on their own. Instead they are encouraged to find a partner to help with the task. Two people carrying a board is relatively easy. But carrying a board on your own can be very difficult. Not only are beginner's boards heavy, finding the way to balance them can be intimidating. Once the women become more accustomed to, and confident in, assessing the best ways to use balance to assist in carrying boards and sails they are often surprised by their own abilities to handle the equipment by themselves. They learn that they can use the wind, instead of fighting it, to help them carry sails and control them on the water. Another instructor within WW emphasised this too:

> Women find problems carrying their board — they're not used to using their bodies that way. (Susan)

Paul, on the other hand explained that it would never have crossed his mind to suggest to anyone learning to windsurf that they should help each other move equipment around. Independence and physical competence are closely associated with masculinity in contrast to physical weakness and incompetence being associated with femininity. The internalisation of learnt feminine attributes is very powerful and can therefore be very inhibiting for women in a way that it is very difficult for those who have not been subject to such lessons to understand. Adele claims that the expectations created on Tuesday evenings, that women will help each other, significantly increases her confidence to both work with others, but also to try things herself, as she no longer worries about failing to prove her independence. Paul now tries to always suggest alternative ways to cope with handling equipment when he is helping on the women's night. However in the past he may have unwittingly created situations similar to one described by Jessica:

> One of the women in particular was so completely put off by having to carry the board down to the beach.... I don't think people realise how tiring it can be, especially if you're not used to physical activity.

Some women are confident in their strength, and some men not. On Tuesday evenings tricks of grip and balance are emphasised so that women do not need to be confident about their strength, instead relying on learnt skills and co-operative behaviour. The transformation of the women's ability to carry and move equipment points to barriers being more to do with learned femininity than with being born a woman.

Lessons on Tuesday evenings take into account that women often approach a physical engagement with timidity, uncertainty and hesitancy. Women tend to lack confidence in their physical abilities (Gill, 1993). Hesitant, fearful body movements are symptomatic of a wider context in which women's bodies are considered objects to be gazed at (Young, 1979, 1980; MacKinnon, 1987). Women employ more energy as they try to overcome being tense, and because they expect little of themselves they do not confidently push themselves. Recent work reveals a patriarchally imposed body movement vocabulary that physically disables and thus oppresses women (Costa and Guthrie, 1994: p. 30).

When a woman recently asked if she could act as my 'apprentice' some evenings, because she was interested in becoming a windsurfing instructor, I passed on the following observation made to me by a woman instructor, and which I have found enlightening and helpful:

> Time and time again the men came along with lots of confident expectations about soon being able to do the fancy tricks they've seen the good sailors do. But the women don't tend to believe that they're ever going to be that good. They start by saying they will be happy if they can just stand on the board... and they get such a buzz when they can actually do things and get so excited and at the end of the course they are so surprised at what they've achieved but the men tend to go away frustrated because they can't do more. (Vanessa)

A group of new women then arrived and I had to stifle a laugh as one said:

> I don't expect to be able to do anything. I will be happy if I can just stay on the board for a while. (Marianne)

As Darlison (1985: p. 55) states:

> For women, the frequent lack of confidence in their own ability, plus the belief that they are simply not capable of performing well, presents a social barrier that is extremely difficult to surmount.

Chipping away at such barriers is an intrinsic component of the supportive approach adopted on Tuesday evenings. This approach may well be attractive to men who do find they are uncomfortable with the association of masculinity with confidence, yet it contrasts with what the women report they have experienced elsewhere:

> When I first tried to windsurf I got so much grief from young chaps- no one seemed interested in helping a rather slow, older woman. (Ros)

> A woman that we sail with, her husband has absolutely no patience with her at all and he just completely and utterly demoralises her and its awful because her confidence is just so completely smashed that she just sails worse and worse all the time. (Kim)

Once an individual woman has gained a skill during a Tuesday evening session she is encouraged to pass it on to someone else. Elitism and concentration on individual prowess is not encouraged. One of the reasons given for participating in a women's event was the support given:

> I was so struck by the women who windsurf really well and weren't out to show off, they couldn't do enough to help you. This is so unusual. My experience with mixed groups is that people who do it really well tend to be dismissive of those of us who are struggling. (Lorraine)

At the lake the women are encouraged to operate a 'buddy system', looking out for each other and sharing any skills and tips that may be appropriate. Women comment, if they have never been before, that they worry the session will be competitive. They are pleasantly surprised to find it to be so supportive and relaxed:

> I just had such a good time and a good laugh. (Olga)

Windsurfing can be competitive but studies have identified that many women avoid that aspect of participation (Birrell, 1994; Scully and Clarke, 1997: p. 27). Outcomes to measure the success of any Tuesday evening session are measured far more by enjoyment than skills acquisition. Sociability is encouraged during women's nights:

> Women seek rapport, support and networking, unlike most men. (Adele)

Socialising is popular before, during, and after the sessions as well as at 'weekends away'. As Kim said:

Being with a group of women is so different and it's really lovely.

It's nice to relax and feel that I don't have to make an effort to look good and to just enjoy being myself and enjoy my windsurfing. (Lisa)

This last quote reflects a more general comment by Jennifer Hargreaves:

Female sports are part of the battle for control of the physical body — an intensely personal process. In western cultures in particular there is a tendency for women to experience their bodies as sites of oppression and to harbour a vision of a different and better body. But sports have become social experiences that for increasing numbers of women are positive, pleasurable and empowering. Women's consciousness about their own physicality is changing and they are active agents in the process. (Hargreaves, 1994: p. 289)

Learning and recognising the strength both of gendered barriers for women and women's individual and collective strength to resist those barriers, especially when given supportive structures, should form a central part of good, anti-discriminatory approaches within all leisure policy and practice. It is easy to overlook the importance of respecting people's own targets for enjoyment, the differing ways people experience and value instrumentality, confidence, safety, risk and challenge and of instructors creating a cooperative atmosphere. Quantitative studies designed to investigate differential participation rates by gender are likewise likely to overlook these issues. The on-going qualitative study, of which this paper forms a part, has produced interesting insights into the lived realities for women, who consciously or not, stretch the boundaries of gender. Once participants started talking, all found they had tales to tell as to how being women affected their experiences windsurfing. Participants also expressed enjoyment exploring the ideas raised. Such studies must provide valuable signposts for positive developments in leisure policy and practice both within and outside the world of windsurfing. Hopefully praxis explored within this paper further encourages myself and others to consider issues of gender and leisure and positive action to take, whether we windsurf or not.

Notes

1   Windsurfing Women can be contacted through Marion Lockey, 37 Hertford, Allerdene, Gateshead, NE9 6DG.

2   Pseudonyms are used throughout to preserve the anonymity of inter-viewees.

References

Allison, L. (1994) *The changing politics of sport*. Manchester: Manchester University Press.

Birrell, S. (1994) 'Women in competitive windsurfing', unpublished project for B. A. Outdoor Education, University of Strathclyde, Glasgow.

Chapman, J. (1993) *Politics, feminism and the reformation of gender*. London: Routledge.

Costa D. M. and Guthrie, S. R. (1994) (eds) *Women and sport*. Champaign, IL: Human Kinetics.

Crawford J., S. Kippax, J. Onynx, U. Gault and P. Benton (1992) *Emotion and gender: Constructing meaning from memory*. London: Sage Publications.

Darlison, L. (1985) 'Women, sport and ideology in Australia', *Fit to play*. Sydney: NSW Women's Advisory Council to the Premier.

Deem, R. (1986) *All work and no play: The sociology of women and leisure*. Open University Press: Milton Keynes.

Gill, D. (1993) 'Psychological, sociological and cultural issues concerning the athletic female', in A. J. Pearl (ed) *The athletic female*. Champaign, IL: Human Kinetics.

Goodale, T. L. and Witt, P. A. (1989) 'Recreation, non-participation and barriers to leisure', in E. L. Jackson and T. L. Burton (eds) *Understanding leisure and recreation. Mapping the past, charting the future*. State College, PA: Venture Publications.

Harding, S. (1991) *Whose science? Whose knowledge? Thinking from women's lives*. Milton Keynes: Open University Press.

Hargreaves, J. (1994) *Sporting females*. London: Routledge.

Hornby, S. (1993) '*Women in coaching*', unpublished action plan, Eastleigh, Hampshire: RYA.

Humberstone, B. (1990) 'Gender, change and adventure education', *Gender and Education* 2: Vol. 2, No. 3: pp. 215–231.

Jackson, S. and Jones, J. (1998) *Contemporary feminist theories*. Edinburgh: Edinburgh University Press.

Kimmel, M. and Messner, M. (eds) (1993) *Men's lives*. New York: Macmillan.

Lather, P (1991) *Getting smart: Feminist research and pedagogy within the postmodern*. London: Routledge.

MacKinnon, C. (1983) Feminism, Marxism, method and the state: Toward a feminist jurisprudence', *Signs* Np. 8: pp. 635–658.

——— (1987) 'Women, self-possession and sport', in *Feminism unmodified*. Cambridge: Harvard University Press.

Mangan, J. A. (1995) 'Sexual Imperatives, Militarism, Mythology, Masculinity', Lecture at Strathclyde University, Glasgow (March).

Olsen, V. (1994) 'Feminisms and models of qualitative research', in N. Denzin and Y. Lincoln (eds) *Handbook of qualitative research*. London: Sage.

Sabo, D. and Gordon, D. (1995) *Men's health and illness: Gender, power and the body*. London: Sage.

Sabo, D. and Runfola, R. (1980) *Jock: Sport and male identity*. Englewood Cliffs NJ Prentice Hall.

Scraton, S. J. (1986) Gender and girls' physical education', *The British Journal of Physical Education* Vol. 17, No. 4: pp. 145–147.

Scully, D. and Clarke, J. (1997) 'Gender issues in sport participation', in J. Kremner, K. Trew and S. Ogle (eds) *Young people's involvement in sport*. London: Routledge.

Talbot, M. (1988) 'Their own worst enemy? Women and leisure provision', in E. Wimbush and M. Talbot (eds) *Relative freedoms: Women and leisure*. Milton Keynes: Open University Press, pp. 161–176.

Theberge, N. (1981) 'A critique of critiques : Radical and feminist writings on sport', *Social Forces* No. 60: p. 2.

Vertinsky, P. A. (1992) Reclaiming space, revisioning the body: The quest for gender sensitive Physical Education', *Quest* No. 44: pp. 373–396.

Wheaton, B. (1998) 'New lads? Risk, challenge and sport participation', paper presented at LSA 4th International Conference "The Big Ghetto: Gender, Sexuality and Leisure", Leeds Metropolitan University (July).

Wimbush, E. and Talbot, M. (eds) (1988) *Relative freedoms*. Milton Keynes: Open University Press.

Woodward, V. (1996) 'Gybing round the buoys', *Trouble and Strife* No. 33 (Summer): pp. 29–34.

——— (1998) 'Being a windsurfing woman', paper to Women in the Community Conference 'Working at Being a Woman', University College Scarborough.

——— (1999) 'Windsurfing women tacking upwind in male infested waters', in M. Terre Blanche and K. K. Bhavanni (eds) *Body politics: Power, knowledge and the body in the social sciences*. South Africa: University of South Africa Press.

Young, I. M. (1979) 'The exclusion of women from sport: Conceptual and existential dimensions philosophy', in *Context* Vol. 9: pp. 44–53.

——— (1980) *Throwing like a girl and other essays in feminist philosophy and social theory*. Bloomington: Indiana University Press.

Women into Outdoor Education: Negotiating a Male-gendered Space — Issues of Physicality

Linda Allin

Division of Sport Sciences, University of Northumbria at Newcastle

Introduction

Outdoor education and outdoor activities have a gendered historical background. The ethos of Kurt Hahn, founder of the Outward Bound movement, was concerned with hard training, physical and mental toughness — elements associated with masculine, rather than feminine identity (Hearn and Morgan, 1990: Messner, 1992). Both Kurt Hahn and Baden Powell, instigator of the Scout movement, were primarily interested in developing the fitness and moral character of *boys*, with particular concern to release male aggressiveness and sexual tensions. Mention of women or girls was, and still is, noticeably absent from outdoor education writings and philosophy (Hogan, 1968; Humberstone, 1994).

Physical activities and sports are also typically classified as 'masculine' or 'feminine' based on the degree of physical challenge, contact and/or risk involved (Kane and Snyder, 1989). According to this categorisation, the outdoor activities at the core of most outdoor education programmes — climbing, expedition work, canoeing and sailing — are generally conceptualised as 'masculine' pursuits. Recent research provides evidence that both male and female physical education teachers still retain traditional views regarding outdoor education in schools as 'male appropriate' activity (Waddington *et al.*, 1998). As such, these activities remain dominated by men, although the numbers of women have been increasing in recent years (Nolan and Priest, 1994). Outdoor education as a career area is also predominantly male, with women particularly underrepresented in the higher levels of outdoor leadership and management (Humberstone, 1994: The Sports Council, 1994).

51

The spaces of outdoor education and outdoor adventurous activities have been, therefore, largely male. This paper presents preliminary findings from life history interviews with 12 prominent women outdoor educators. The research focuses on their work and recreational experiences as they negotiated their way from the recreational level of outdoor activities through to the occupational level (Loeffler, 1995). Due to the significance of the sporting body as the site of constructing and negotiating identities (Hall, 1996) and the centrality of outdoor activities to their life stories (compare Armour, 1997; Sparkes, 1996) this paper highlights the role of the physical dimension. The aim of this investigation, for the purpose of this paper, has been to explore the women's relationships with their physical selves and the influence of their physicality in negotiating male dominated outdoor careers. In understanding their physicality in this context it became impossible to disentangle connections with masculinity, femininity and sexuality.

Physicality and outdoor education

McDermott (1996) provides a useful review of the notion of physicality. In her article, she points out that:

> ... perhaps most commonly, physicality is linked to power, but for the most part, these discussions are related to male physical power and masculinity. (p. 13)

Messner (1992) and Connell (1987) argue that boys construct their masculine identity through their experiences of sport. Messner (1992), in speaking of his research into the lives of athletes, also noted that the lack of women in sport was influential in his interviewees' absorption of the values and physical nature of sports as part of masculine identity:

> The fact that sport was an exclusively male world made it seem natural to equate masculinity with competition, physical strength and skills. (p. 31)

Later, Messner equates the embodiment of masculinity with the physical nature of sport in terms of aggression, physical challenge and potential for injury. It is on this basis of physicality that sports have also been classified as 'masculine' or 'feminine'. Thus, as noted above, the majority of outdoor pursuits have assumed a masculine label and a 'macho' image. This image, it is suggested, ultimately constrains women's participation in such activities through suggesting that involvement requires being 'unfeminine', 'butch' or 'becoming a man'. Crawley (1998), also suggests that unnecessarily emphasising the physical requirements of outdoor pursuits (in her case, sailing) only serves to exclude most women and so maintains the 'natural superiority' of males in such activities. A lack of participation by women then reinforces the notion of the activity and its characteristics as masculine.

The increasing numbers of women involved in outdoor activities, however, suggests that it is becoming less relevant to understand the term physicality as synonymous with the embodiment of hegemonic masculinity and/or male power. Feminist and postmodern thinking also now centres on fragmented identities and subjectivities in women's lives (see Hollinger, 1994: Bloom and Munro, 1995). In investigating the lives and experiences of women, there is awareness of different ways in which physically active women relate to their physical selves. As McDermott (1996: p. 17) illustrates:

> From my own experiences as a physically active woman, with a resulting well-grounded understanding of the capabilities of my body, I use the term physicality within my own life experiences. And from this understanding of it, I am led to reject the idea that sporting physicality only relates to particular kinds of male power and/or masculinity, as well as to specific kinds of actions, skills or sports. In other words, this particular interpretation does not relate to my lived, physically active, bodily experiences as a female.

This paper examines the lived experiences of twelve women who are, by the very fact of their having followed careers in outdoor education, unrepresentative of the majority of women. The issue of their *physicality*, in the sense of simply *how they experience themselves physically*, becomes an important one for understanding the ways in which they have managed their outdoor careers and identities. It needs also to be recognised that their experiences of physicality take place within a context of gender relations in an activity which is defined as masculine and dominated by men. Thus the issues of gender identity, power and control remain highly important. This is particularly as the body may be seen the "site in which conflicts about gender identity and professional identity are often controlled and negotiated" (Bloom and Munro, 1995: p. 100).

The research process

The material for this research comes from in-depth interviews from 12 women, taken as part of ongoing research into the lives and careers of women in outdoor education. Two women were contacted initially from the Association of Mountaineering Instructors membership list. Two others were obtained through the British Canoe Union Handbook as women sufficiently qualified to run their own outdoor courses. By obtaining names in this way it was considered that these women would be fairly highly qualified women who were using those qualifications professionally. Those chosen were also names familiar to me as prominent women in outdoor education. Future respondents were contacted through a 'snowballing' effect, whereby those women interviewed would give me the names of other women they knew who were involved in outdoor education. As several people mentioned the same names, those women would be considered for interview. The reason for this was partly due to the 'outdoor world' being a small, interconnected one. It was also due to the relatively few numbers of prominent women in outdoor education and the difficulty in locating them easily without contacting outdoor establishments individually. Each woman was then sent a letter outlining the nature of the research, asking for preliminary career history information and asking whether they would be willing to give up the time to be interviewed. Only one woman contacted refused permission as she would be on maternity leave from her current post and did not consider that she would have sufficient time. Interviews mostly took place either in the respondent's home or a workplace. Two interviews were undertaken in a quiet café.

I was interested in the lives of the women outdoor educators as they related to their careers in outdoor education. Interviewees were invited to discuss any life or work issues and experiences pertinent to them. In most instances interviews began with an invitation to 'tell me something about your family background, and go from there'. Although this was an arbitrary starting point in time, the stories of some interviewees moved forwards and backwards in time according to the significance of particular issues and their memories. The decision to leave the main content of the interview open for the interviewee was based on the exploratory nature of the research. Towards the end of initial interviews and earlier in the interviews as they progressed, I offered some of my own experiences and background and the interviews became more conversational. It was my concern to be seen as somebody genuinely interested in their stories rather than someone exploiting the interview situation (see Oakley, 1981 and Stanley, 1983 for discussions concerning power relations). My self-presentation to interviewees as a woman who has been involved in outdoor education and is still active in outdoor activities helped in establishing a relationship with the majority of interviewees. However, it would be naive to think that this addressed all the issues concerned with the researcher-researched relationship. Interviewees were asked for permission to tape record the conversations. Interviews lasted approximately two hours.

Data analysis was begun soon after the collection of the first four interviews and is being undertaken in accordance with an inductive, grounded theory approach (Glaser and Strauss, 1967). Thus it is an ongoing process with modification and development as further interviews and analysis take place. Each interview gained so far has been transcribed onto a word processor and read through repeatedly. The procedure followed that advocated by Maykut and Moorhouse, (1994) and was similar to the 'open coding' of Strauss and Corbin (1990) in that transcripts have been indexed, notes scribbled alongside and pieces of text representing an idea or segment of meaning have been labelled. There has been continual comparison between later and early interviews. Transitions and turning points have been identified. The main concern in this phase was to make the fullest sense of the data and emerging themes. For this paper, I have pulled out from the transcripts quotations which seem to illustrate different aspects of physicality and the body. In trying to interview women who might provide variation on emerging themes, women of different ages, employment positions and family circumstances have been sought. At the time of writing, data analysis and collection are still in progress and findings must be regarded as preliminary.

The women interviewed have not seen the sense I have been making of their stories. This paper must be read, therefore, as *my* representation and interpretation of their experiences. It has been my choice to focus on the physical dimension, my choice of extracts to include or disregard. In doing this, I am aware of the dilemmas associated with having this power (see Harrison and Lyon, 1993; Clarke and Humberstone, 1997; Dewar, 1991; Sparkes, 1995). Although I have acknowledged rather than overcome these issues, for presentation I use the interviewees' own words to illustrate their experiences. As my searches for black or lesbian women in outdoor education have so far proved difficult, in this paper I may also be accused of generally presenting the experiences of white, heterosexual women (Dewar, 1993).

The women in outdoor education

The women interviewed were aged between 34 and 61 years. One woman identified herself as black, all others were white. They came from a variety of working and middle class family backgrounds, although the majority came from upbringings which encouraged and supported achievement for women. All have been involved with outdoor education for ten years or more They had varied histories in outdoor recreation prior to their outdoor education employment or training. The early experiences of these women must therefore be located in a historical time period where there were few women involved in outdoor activities or employment. Five women had children and one woman was pregnant at the time of interview. Some were married, some single and two with children were divorced. They were working in a number of different contexts; local authority outdoor education centres, higher education, charity run establishments and self-employed. The women have been allocated initials to protect their identities.

Physicality, masculinity, femininity

Nearly all the women had early outdoor experiences of an informal nature. For many, this involved camping holidays with the family, hillwalking or simply adventure play in an outdoor environment. Many women specifically mentioned male encouraging influences such as fathers, brothers or male playmates. The majority of interviewees then became highly involved in traditional school sporting activities, frequently to a competitive level, with one third going on from school to become PE teachers. Only K described herself as unsporty in the traditional sense — "anything with a ball, you can forget it". The women in this study were therefore already gaining knowledge about their physical selves through their activities and their relationships with significant others. They frequently had support and encouragement from home and school and enjoyed using their bodies. B stresses how much she enjoyed exercise and exerting herself physically:

> And I've always enjoyed exerting myself, I *enjoy* exercise, and so the thing of doing something like take this absurdly wobbly boat down rapids and technical water was just a tremendous challenge.

In similar vein, the following comment illustrates how M felt that her physical qualities helped her to participate, achieve and progress in a male dominated outdoor sport without feeling marginalised as the only female in the group:

> It was fine, you know, I mean we were pretty fit, I've always had a lot of stamina and been quite fit, so I've always coped, you know ... and it never occurred to me, well it probably did occur to me, but it never bothered me that I was the only woman ... and it's where it's come from really, you know I've always felt that I could hold my own and that's probably the difference.

Several others also particularly identified themselves as strong or fit women who were therefore able to perform well at outdoor activities and 'hold their own' in a male dominated physical environment. This was even though most of the women interviewed appeared to be of quite small and slim build. One noted how she just had to "use her body really well — as everyone ought to" and that "brute strength doesn't come into it".

Most women did not necessarily identify their physical qualities with being masculine, yet two identified themselves as 'tomboys' and others used phrases to suggest they perceived themselves as 'not typical' women. Thus there was evidence of internalisation of common notions of masculine/feminine, similar to that found by Sisjord (1997) with female wrestlers. S suggested that she had developed a more 'masculine' identity through her time spent in a male outdoor environment. Soon after her comment concerning her physical strength she continued:

> I feel I developed quite a few of the male type of traits if you like, or characteristics, going through a career like this which is very male dominated. It's just a philosophy of mine, but because of my up-bringing or the influences in my life, they've often been male in terms of the outdoor things, they taught me, and people I've done things with, I've been a little more that way inclined than the feminine traits one might expect from a woman.

None of the other women so openly expressed their interpretations in this way. However, M noted that in her early career she "wore chequered shirts so I could be like the men and I never had long hair even though I find it easier in the outdoors to have long hair because I can tie it back". L also illustrated how her University canoe club maintained a physically masculine culture which served to exclude women from entry:

> And they didn't allow women in the canoe club — you could do a course with the department of physical education but the whitewater club was very elitist really, and I mean you weren't allowed to wear wetsuits, or not not allowed, but it wasn't the done thing, you wore damart and shorts and there weren't any women basically.

L was eventually accepted into the club through association with her boyfriend and the competence she had developed by kayaking with him. She talked of her first trip with the club as an 'epic', whereby she ended up badly bruised following a capsize, but she ended the story, "and that was it, hooked on kayaking". Others noted similar 'adventure' experiences. Indeed, it was when talking about their adventures and risks that the interviewees really became animated and enthusiastic in the interview situation. H noted "it was either learn to roll or forget it!".

From the above comments it appears that showing a strong sense of their physical qualities and finding enjoyment in extending their physical abilities helped these women to negotiate the recreational level of outdoor pursuits. Women did not tend to identify their sense of physicality with being masculine though many had a typically male 'get stuck in' attitude to the adventurous elements of the activities (compare Young, 1997; Young and White, 1995). However, women were generally aware of and accepted the fact that they were negotiating a male/masculine environment. In order to be accepted, some women found they managed their physical identities in order to comply with the dominant male culture.

Physical confidence

Within the interviews it was highly surprising to find so many very competent outdoor women who expressed themselves as lacking in physical confidence in their early careers. This was despite a confident outward appearance. H noted her lack of confidence as a "typically female thing". Many interviewees stressed the support and encouragement they had received from significant men in their lives. Several women specifically mentioned how having encouraging male partners or colleagues who were highly skilled helped enhance their self-perceptions and skill development. B, for example, said:

> Most people now see me as quite a confident person, but I was actually quite lacking in confidence myself and there's no doubt about it the fact that he could look after me in any outdoor situation was a big plus for me, and even though I now recognise that I underestimated my own abilities, I was just reassured by him being there and like he could always pick up the pieces.

These women were all technically highly competent, yet at times their words also reveal images of being 'looked after' or protected. It was noticeable that none of the women interviewed exceeded their male partners in terms of overall skill levels in canoeing or climbing. Findings such as these demonstrate that although these women have challenged their expected roles in becoming highly physically skilled in outdoor activities, it seems that many of them did so in contexts which may be more likely to reproduce gender stereotypes. As a further illustration of this, K described how the structure of her teacher-training course also preserved hierarchical gender relations:

> And the way it was worked was kind of an apprenticeship set up if you like, where people were in different groups according to ability and the

> more experienced would teach the less experienced in particular areas. The problem was that there [was no] woman who had a higher skill level than the men on the activities and so the women were always being taught by the men.

This finding supports Scraton (1992) and Flintoff (1996) in noting that teaching practices and structures in physical educational establishments often serve to reproduce rather than challenge gender stereotypes. Many women had also accepted the structure of the outdoors as it was. S commented:

> ... because it's been a male dominated thing and you just accept that most of the people on any course and the instructors are going to be male ... but that hasn't ever bothered me at all.

Being involved in outdoor activities in a predominantly male group was not therefore generally perceived as openly constraining. However, there was some evidence that it might have a subtle effect on confidence levels. The following example illustrates the experiences of W, who went on to become involved in women only groups:

> Let's just say you are getting ready to go out and they say 'do you really think you can handle a force five?' — and you know that, you're getting yourself ready and you're perfectly confident you can do it, but by them saying are you sure you can handle it, or 'do you not think that sail's a bit too big for these conditions', or 'phew, it's really hairy out there', or 'are you sure you want to be going out?' and mostly what you need is confidence, to just go out there knowing you can hang out and just do it and if you're the slightest bit wobbly then of course the sail will take you and you're not going to be able to do it ... and just little things like that, and you try and get yourself hardened up to it, but I do find myself doubting, even though you are probably better than they are anyway ....

This point perhaps illustrates how a 'male' environment and language can undermine as well as enhance women's confidence in their physical selves. In this, it perhaps suggests the need for women to develop skill and confidence in different contexts. For example, most women said that they enjoyed doing activities with other women and that the experience differed from their experiences with men. Though as C put it:

it isn't so much the differences as the similarities ... without consciously thinking about it, that person is not better because they are stronger ... I can't say 'oh she can do it because she's stronger, or she can do it because she is taller than me ... because she isn't! ... that's why I think we push each other along ... again its the supportive (element).

This was a significant point as it suggests that physical differences between the sexes in attributes perceived to be important in outdoor activities may lead to decreased motivation and expectations of success. Perhaps the increase in numbers of women in the activities may therefore be liberating in allowing women to recognise and use their own physicality through challenging the limitations they may put on their abilities in a mixed environment.

Tensions in a physically masculine working environment

The research did find evidence of tensions and struggles in the working environment. It was significant that in most cases the basis for tensions and conflicts were rooted in the demonstration of male physicality. That is, women felt most uncomfortable when the environment was perceived as 'macho' or unnecessarily emphasised elements associated with masculine identity, such as physical performance, skill or endurance (Messner, 1992). The following extracts show how different women experienced tensions as they negotiated their way through their careers and how some resolved these tensions by choosing alternative career pathways. One woman, from a traditionally working class upbringing and working in an inner city charity environment commented:

There are loads of times, loads of times that I would say that I've been held down, loads of times ... and I think I was struggling more with the issues of being a woman in a male environment than actually going for qualifications.

This contrasted with the other women interviewed, who did not perceive deliberate discrimination in the male environment. Indeed all women perceived advantages for themselves in terms of employment opportunities, although at times they were not certain whether they had obtained the job by virtue of their sex or their skills. In reflecting on her entry to outdoor pursuits leadership at a very traditional school, B did face direction opposition. However, she particularly highlighted how the emphasis on authoritarian leadership, hard training and physicality caused her concern:

> I just realised that I worked in completely different ways than the other guys who worked in a way of if you can't cope with the pace then forget it, and they had girls in tears ... the paddling was very endurance based paddling and it was if you can't cope with this then bad luck, we're not slowing down for you sort of thing, and oh if you can't run up the steps to the castle ... 'cause the ethos was on this hard training, which me being pretty physical, I loved ... and I think it was, I think I very naively, I suppose I managed well at things because I was strong, because I could do things I didn't think it was a barrier and what I hadn't realised at all was really how big the barrier was ... and what I saw was designed to destroy people's confidence, it was designed to make people feel inadequate, and it reduced the numbers of women far more than it reduced the numbers of men.

In this instance, the conflict with her personal values and more caring ways of working resulted in B's decision to leave the beach rescue unit. Notice that her own strong sense of her physical self which had contributed to her enjoyment of the recreational level also contributed to her naivety in terms of gender issues. The impact of the teaching style on confidence and the numbers of women remaining in the activity is also significant. The interaction between physical confidence and the male environment is highlighted through the experiences of L and A. L described her feelings as the only female working in a well known outdoor centre:

> it was interesting ... I think I felt a bit insecure as though I wasn't really a good enough performer to be there ... I knew I had good people skills, I knew that I worked very well with people and was a good teacher, but I wasn't even confident enough about that to tell other people ... nobody really asked kind of where I was coming from, and actually I'd had quite a colourful life but I hadn't climbed Everest or led Left Wall or whatever I needed, I felt I needed to get credibility at (the centre) ... but it was quite strange because on a Monday morning it was oh well what routes did you lead at the weekend you know, and often I couldn't say anything, and loads of the conversations and stuff were about routes and I could never remember the names of routes, so it was a struggle in some ways.

Here, too, it seemed that the culture emphasised visible achievements and high physical technical abilities — areas in which L felt unsure. Although L was aware that she was a good teacher, it appeared that despite being of great importance, it was not openly valued. The staffroom space was also dominated by conversations concerning performance and demonstration of skill — elements associated with masculine identity (Paetcher and Head, 1996). This, and the apparent lack of interaction on a more personal level, contributed to L's sense of marginalisation. A, who had worked at the same centre some years previously, told a different story:

> I mean I just got on very well with them, I never felt, never felt any discrimination and I never have done in all the time I worked in the outdoors, you know, people say we're put down and this and that, but I never actually felt this at all ... but I mean I suppose not many of them have been to the Himalayas or climbed anything, which did put me at a slight advantage I suppose.

However, A also noted that:

> I would never have gone and worked in a situation like that without having gone away and achieved what we had done in that year, and I think it did give me confidence.

Thus it seemed that her past achievement experiences had impacted on her experiences at the centre. At the same time comments by K showed that the actual physical demands of outdoor pursuits employment at the highest level combined with a 'macho' image, also served to deter women from applying for certain positions. She says of another high performance centre:

> I think it's 'cause women don't want to work there, I wouldn't want to work there, and certainly working there in winter you are just physically challenged all the time and out in very arduous conditions and it also, I don't know if it still does, but (the centre) did have quite a reputation for not being very welcoming or comfortable environment for women working there.

Some women, therefore, had still perceived discomfort in an elite male working environment. Generally, however, there were perceptions that the macho element in the outdoor environment might be changing and that women's increased participation in the outdoors was helping this. As M said:

> ... the more women you get I think it will blow the macho cover, the same at the C centre, there are two women there now and I mean there's a lot of wit and repartee there, but a lot of it is male piss-taking

and it's just sort of taken the macho element of that, I mean the humour is still there.

There were therefore perceptions that increasing the number of women in outdoor education employment might eventually lead to a more comfortable and supportive working environment for both women and men.

Physicality, pregnancy and sexuality

One of the most significant aspects of physicality experienced by women is that of pregnancy and childbirth. Similarly, presenting such a masculine environment with female physicality in its most visible form may be considered a great challenge to existing norms. Five of the interviewees in this research had children and one was pregnant at the time of interview. The following section illustrates the ways in which the women managed their pregnancy at work and in their outdoor recreation.

Several women interviewed had made decisions not to have children, some on the basis that it was not compatible with their outdoor lives and they would feel frustrated or hampered. L, at the time of interview was struggling internally with a desire for children versus the impact this might have on her developing skill in an outdoor sport. As she ended:

> ... and I think it's my (outdoor activity) as much as anything. I know (the activity) is incompatible with being pregnant.

This contrasted with B, whose confidence in her physical self enabled her to challenge the common perception of pregnancy as something necessarily means the end or interruption of a physical career. She explained:

> I raced the (international competition) when I was three months pregnant and nobody knew. I was feeling very sick a lot of the time, but I raced and trained and I paddled the day before I had (my child) and I paddled again three days later I think ... but I was very fit and healthy.

In contrast, M, who has two children, illustrated how the complex relationships between pregnancy, physicality and the male professional environment led to her restricting her own career moves. She commented:

> Permanent jobs came up here which I thought well I wouldn't apply for really, 'cause I want another child and although I had an excellent

pregnancy with B, I could get morning sickness coming to work, saying, 'oh I can't take them up the hill today you know' and the way the centre was then it was all male staff and I didn't feel I could do that ... now in retrospect I would do it now ... but then being a woman in a centre you thought you had to do as well as the men, you couldn't afford to let down, you couldn't have them say 'oh that's because she's a woman instructor, they'll all behave like that ....

This extract vividly illustrates the internal pressures and conflicts placed upon M as an early representative of women in the male world of outdoor education. If she took sick leave, she was succumbing to the 'pregnancy as illness' perception which has historically served to constrain the physical activities of women. If she remained at work, but worked less than 100%, she would be contributing to the perception that women in general were not committed to or able to work in an outdoor environment. By choosing not to apply for a permanent position at this stage, M was at least able to have some control over her actions, although it meant putting her own career on hold. J, in contrast, challenged perceptions by working whilst visibly pregnant:

It wasn't an easy time really, because nobody knew what I could and couldn't do, and then Health and Safety was banded around and everyone was conscious that maybe a big, fat pregnant woman wasn't the person to be around ... my doctor got involved and suggested that after 20 weeks it wasn't a good idea for me to be doing things that could damage my back, like canoeing or rockclimbing, so that meant I could do field work like the walking and then I made the decision myself that I would finish at 29 weeks, 'cause I got the impression that they didn't want me around — I was getting too fat! ... and they thought I was a bit of a liability.

Confronting the traditionally male space with the physical aspects of pregnancy therefore caused confusion and upheaval. However J also commented that getting married and having a baby marked a strangely positive change in her working environment.

And they see D when (my husband) comes to pick me up and there's pictures round the centre and things, and I think it has enhanced our working environment, there are other things to talk about, it's enhanced my relationship with men, members of staff which I didn't think it would ... men just want to talk about their children basically and I think before they used to think I was a bit of an automaton and just one of those strange women that did outdoory things ....

For J, the 'feminising' of the work environment through family photographs made the workplace a more relaxed place to be. As J put, "it was quite bizarre, it like humanises you"; perhaps that should read "it feminises you". Like the female bodybuilder, perhaps women in the outdoors are "difficult to position" in terms of traditionally ascribed notions of the feminine (Hall, 1996: p. 60). It was significant in her story that J received less support from her female head of centre who "found it all a bit strange, babies and all that". This suggests that it is not necessarily differences between the sexes which can create tensions, but rather differences in the images and perceptions of women in the outdoors and their femininity/sexuality in the working outdoor environment.

Concluding comments

This paper hints at the role of physicality in the work and recreational experiences of 12 women as they negotiated their way through the male space of outdoor education careers. The findings suggest a complicated picture of physicality, masculinity/femininity, and sexuality. Women both resisted and conformed to gender stereotypes at different times. For example, while they generally accepted and accommodated to male structures (passive) they also used their relationships with their physical selves to challenge the traditional expectations of women's capabilities (active). Their physical qualities were not seen as necessarily masculine, but rather as a source of agency in negotiating a male environment. Yet some had rejected notions of femininity by saying they were not typical women and some had altered their physical identities to fit in with a male culture. Many revealed an early lack of physical confidence which was identified as 'typically female'. There was also evidence of tensions and struggles in an environment constructed as physically masculine. The presence of other women was welcomed, yet women in positions of power did not necessarily identify with or support other women. These are areas which need to be explored.

The women in this study have lived and worked through the last 20-30 years in a context where almost all at some stage found themselves the only woman in their recreational or professional environment. It was also a context which has seen changing ideas and expectations concerning physically active women. The collection of data now goes forward to include younger women who are just gaining entry to the occupational level of outdoor education. The research will continue to develop findings concerning the influence and meanings of physicality and the body to women's lives and careers in outdoor education. The research so far also suggests that there needs to be a concerted effort to investigate further experiences of women who differ in class upbringing, 'race' and sexuality.

References

Armour, K. (1997) 'Developing a personal philosophy on the nature and purpose of physical education: Life history reflections', *European Physical Education Review* Vol. 3, No. 1: pp. 68–82.

Bloom, R. L. and Munro, P. (1995) 'Conflicts of selves; Nonunitary subjectivity in women administrators' life history narratives', in J. A. Hatch and R. Wisniewski (eds) *Life history and narrative*. Qualitative Studies Series One. London: Falmer Press.

Clarke, G. and Humberstone, B. (1997) 'Managing women's sport organisations', in Clarke, G. and Humberstone, B. (eds) *Researching women and sport*. London: Macmillan Press.

Connell, R. (1987) *Gender and power*. Stanford: Stanford University Press.

Crawley, S. (1998) 'Gender, class and the construction of masculinity in professional sailing', *International Review for the Sociology of Sport* Vol. 33, No. 1: pp. 33–42.

Dewar, A. (1991) 'Feminist pedagogy in physical education: Promises, possibilities and pitfalls', *Journal of Physical Education, Recreation and Dance* Vol. 62, No. 6: pp. 68–77.

Dewar, D. (1993) 'Would all generic women in sport please stand up? Challenges facing feminist sport sociology', *Quest* Vol. 45, No. 2: pp. 211–229.

Flintoff, A. (1996) 'We have no problems with equal opportunities here ....We've got mixed changing rooms', *The British Journal of Physical Education*, Spring 1996: pp. 21–23.

Glaser, B and Strauss, A (1967) 'The discovery of grounded theory', cited in A. Strauss and J. Corbin, *Basics of qualitative research: Grounded theory procedures and techniques*. London: Sage.

Hall, A. (1996) *Feminism and sporting bodies, Essays on theories and practice*. Leeds: Human Kinetics.

Harrison B. and Lyon, S. (1993) 'A note on ethical issues in the use of autobiography in sociological research', *Sociology* Vol. 27, No. 1: pp. 101–109.

Hearn, J and Morgan, D. (1990) *Men, masculinities and social theory*. London: Unwin.

Hollinger, R (1994) 'Postmodernism and the social sciences alternative approach', *Contemporary Social Theory Volume 4*. London: Sage.

Hogan, J. M. (1968) *Impelled into experiences: The story of the Outward Bound schools*. London and Wakefield: Educational Productions.

Humberstone, B. (1994) 'Gender and outdoor education', *Perspectives in Education*, University of Exeter 50: pp. 80–93.

Kane, M. J. and Snyder E. (1989) 'Sport typing: The social "containment" of women in sport', *Arena Review* Vol. 13, No. 2: pp. 77–96.

Loeffler, T. A. (1995) 'Factors influencing women's outdoor leadership career development', *Melpomene Journal* Vol. 14, No. 93: pp. 15–21.

Maykut, P. and Morehouse, R. (1994) *Beginning qualitative research. A philosophic and practical guide*. London: Falmer Press.

McDermott, L. (1996) 'Toward a feminist understanding of physicality within the context of women's physically active and sporting lives', *Sociology of Sport Journal* 13: pp. 12–30.

Messner, M. (1992) *Power at play, sport and the problem of masculinity*. Boston: Beacon Press.

Nolan, T. and Priest, S. (1994) 'Outdoor programmes for women only', *Journal of Adventure Education and Outdoor Leadership* Vol. 10, No. 1: pp. 14–17.

Oakley, A. (1981) 'Women interviewing women: A contradiction in terms', in H. Roberts (ed) *Doing feminist research*. London: Routledge.

Paetcher, C. and Head, J. (1996) 'Gender, identity, status and the body: Life in a marginal subject', *Gender and Education* Vol. 8, No. 1: pp. 21–29.

Scraton, S. (1992) *Shaping up to womanhood: gender and girls' physical educatiopn*. Buckingham: Open University Press.

Sisjord, M. (1997) 'Wrestling with gender', *International Review for the Sociology of Sport* Vol. 32, No. 4: pp. 433–438.

Sparkes, A. (1995) 'Writing people: Reflections on the dual crisis of representation and legitimation in qualitative inquiry', *Quest*, 47: pp. 158–195.

Sparkes, A. (1996) 'The fatal flaw: A narrative of the fragile body self', *Qualitative Inquiry* Vol. 2, No. 4: pp. 463–494.

Sports Council (1994)*Women in coaching: The Governing Body perspective.* London: The Sports Council.

Stanley, L. (1983) *Feminist praxis.* London: Routledge.

Stevenson, C. (1990) 'The early careers of international athletes', *Sociology of Sport Journal* 7: pp. 238–253.

Strauss, A. and Corbin. J. (1990) *Basics of qualitative research. Grounded theory procedures and techniques.* London: Sage.

Waddington, I. (1998) 'Gender stereotyping and physical education', *European Physical Education Review* Vol. 4, No. 1: pp. 34–46.

Young, K. (1997) 'Women, sport and physicality', *International Review of Sport Sociology* Vol. 32, No. 3: pp. 297–305.

Young, K. and White, P. (1995) 'Sport, physical danger and injury; The experience of elite women athletes', *Journal of Sport and Social Issues*, 19: pp. 45–61.

Developing Confidence in Women Working Outdoors: An Exploration of Self Confidence and Competence in Women Employed in Adventure Recreation

May Carter

**School of Marketing, Tourism and Leisure,
Edith Cowan University, Australia**

In early 1985, I stood on the bank of a river in south east Queensland, watching friends make their way through a long, tumbling rapid. I was feeling exhilarated because I had just managed to paddle my kayak through, even though some of my journey was backwards! I had spent a lot of time outdoors but it was the first time I had achieved anything like that. As I watched the others, I saw their faces change from fright as they entered the rapid, to delight as they hit the flat water at the end. I knew that feeling and I relived it with each one of them. Standing there, I decided that I really wanted to do this for a living. It didn't matter how or where, I was going to leave my boring office job and I was going to work outdoors.

That was over ten years ago. Of those ten years working in the field, I have spent the past five years running my own small adventure recreation business. The outdoor programmes offered by my business were simple, fun and designed to be accessible to as many people as possible. Initially, I enjoyed my time working outdoors, but by the end, I was tired, felt dispirited, lacking in confidence and unsure of my competence in so many areas of outdoor skill. The physical demands of working in the adventure industry were one thing, the emotional demands were far harder to deal with. I felt I had to keep proving my ability and knowledge over and over again. My methods were, at times, ridiculed by my peers, or dismissed as just that "girly" stuff, as they placed more emphasis on enjoying, and not conquering, the outdoors. I felt my opinions and input were often ignored by my male colleagues, even by one male employee who was dependent on my hand to sign his pay cheque! My self esteem was the lowest it had ever been. I felt I had

nothing to offer and nowhere to go in the adventure recreation industry. I
could no longer cope with the work of being outdoors and decided to return
to post graduate study. I needed time to re-evaluate my professional life and
take stock of what I had achieved.

This paper itself is as much an exercise in personal exploration as an
academic discussion. When I began to speak with women employed in the
adventure recreation field, as research for my post graduate thesis, I noted an
undercurrent of uncertainty and lack of confidence expressed by several of the
women. It was most apparent when they were talking about their skills as
outdoor instructors and the position they held within the adventure industry.
I realised I was not alone in feeling less than confident about my ability. I also
began to wonder if the problem I had identified was related more to a lack of
identity and a sense of belonging, than assessment of ability.

This paper explores the position of women who have chosen to seek
employment within the adventure recreation industry. It is proposed that
despite the high level of skill attained by many women within the industry,
they continue to question their own ability. In a recent study of North
American women's career development in outdoor leadership, eighty-four per
cent of the women who participated, described how a lack of self confidence
in their abilities limited them in pursuing promotion and recognition (Loeffler,
1997). In the same study, male respondents identified women's perception of
themselves as less qualified and competent as the major constraint to their
advancement within the industry (Loeffler, 1995).

This chapter discusses the attitudes and practices that exist within the
adventure recreation industry in Australia and the effect these have on the
perception of women and their place within the industry. It is proposed that
very little will happen to improve the position of women until the traditional
masculinist attitudes and practices of the adventure recreation industry are
replaced with gender equitable alternatives. In addition, women must find
ways to recognise the value of their skills and objectively assess their level of
competency. More importantly, women must maintain their self esteem by
insisting on the acceptance of their legitimate right to explore and enact their
own ways of working in the outdoors.

The findings of international research, and my own research in progress,
are discussed in an effort to explore the issue of self confidence in women
working outdoors. This chapter presents several changes in approach to
industry training that may improve the working life of women outdoors. I hope
that by opening up discussion, more people will realise how important it is for
the adventure recreation industry to see beyond the traditional masculinist
stereotypes of adventure, and believe that women can be capable, competent
outdoor professionals.

It's a man's world! Or is it?

Until recently, most published material on adventure recreation presented adventure from a primarily "malestream" perspective (Stockham, 1996). Outdoor adventure is described as a male domain in that the experience is "male defined and male dominated" (Knapp, 1985: p. 16). The tendency to por-tray adventure in terms of heroic quests and brave endeavours harks back to the early connection of adventure pursuits in education and training to military models. The most obvious of these connections is the early Outward Bound School model, established in the United Kingdom in 1941. The Outward Bound School was developed to provide life and survival skill training for young men (Miner, 1990). Women were not initially considered as candidates for Outward Bound training, until the astonishing discovery that girls could handle the same courses with the same degree of difficulty as boys. The continuing percep-tion that women do not have a legitimate place in military training is evident. Recent Australian research found that sexual harassment of female military recruits was rife, even at the elite Defence Force Academy (Hawes *et al.*, 1998).

Historically, the contributions of women and the specific benefits of adventure for women were largely ignored. Women commonly accompanied men in the outdoors but their accomplishments were obscured in the literature as they were relegated to the role of helpmate. Women's achievements in adventure recreation were often questioned or minimised (Bialeschki, 1992). The concept of women in the outdoors holds a degree of curiosity value or conjures up images of "rough and tough individuals" (Henderson, 1992, p.49).

The expectation that employment in the adventure recreation industry will involve long periods away from home, a high level of physical activity and the real possibility of injury, often removes employment in this field from the realm of career opportunities traditionally offered to young women. Outdoor leadership requires women to exist outside traditional indoor employment roles and contrary to social expectations that they will be home based carers and nurturers. Loeffler (1995: p. 26) found that women seeking careers in the adventure recreation industry often faced social sanctions and stigma, including the derogatory labelling of strong, competent women as lesbian. Humberstone (1996) feels the continuing general perception that adventure is inappropriate for women has resulted in a lack of women seeking career paths within this industry.

The predominance of male employees in the adventure recreation field has created a tradition of masculine control that excludes women from key positions. Loeffler (1995) identified the "old boy network" as the greatest barrier faced by North American women in developing careers in outdoor leadership. Women felt that there was discrimination in hiring and training and that they were excluded from informal male networks. To add a further degree of difficulty, very few women "got in on the ground floor" of organisations instituted in the 1970s and 1980s. Consequently, few women hold key positions in established adventure recreation organisations where they can influence policy and decision making that takes into account women's needs.

One of the other many reasons given for the lack of women in adventure recreation employment was an over-emphasis on the teaching of technical or activity (hard) skills and an under emphasis of the teaching of people (soft) skills in outdoor leadership training programs. It was felt that the expectation of high levels of technical competency was male driven, so that when women were measured against these standards, they often failed (Loeffler, 1995). These feelings were discussed in a study conducted by Green (1994) with tertiary students of outdoor education in Victoria, Australia. The young women interviewed in this study proposed that without personal traits such as compassion, insight, empathy and good social and interpersonal skills, instructors in the outdoors were "useless" (Green, 1994: p. 28). However, they believed personal skills were often overlooked and, as women, their level of technical skill was devalued. The perception of strength seemed to play a more important role in determining who was a competent outdoor instructor. One of Green's participants summed it up this way:

> Strength and skill are two different things. Women with good technique do well but they are compared to men with strength. The strength factor overtakes the skill factor — from messages we receive, we assume that we physically have to be behind the guys. In general, the guys in outdoor education don't view women as equal in terms of physical activity and skill ... it comes back to the strength thing ... guys are at a higher skill level. (p. 28)

Green's (1994) study also found that even though the young women felt confident about their ability, they were often not taken seriously by their male counterparts, again largely due to physical comparisons on performance. This constant comparison sets up an intriguing paradox. On one hand the women claimed they were competent in their technical skills yet they continued to receive messages that they were not up to "standard", a standard established by the male students. It is worth considering what would happen if these young women put their own approach first. Rather than seeing strength as the determining factor in competence, it may well be that the ability to balance the technical and personal skills is, in fact, a more appropriate standard of competence for the adventure recreation industry to adopt.

The perception of lack of ability confronted these young women again when they took on leadership roles. The women believed they were capable of being competent leaders but external factors made the task difficult. Most often it was the belief by some males that women did not belong in outdoor leadership because the role was too physical and too demanding. Again, the determining factor for good leadership was based on physical strength. The assumption that strength is a key element in good leadership is contrary to much research. Knapp (1985) discusses approaches to successful management and leadership as involving intuition, cooperation and teamwork, traits often associated with women. Green (1994) reports that the women were clearly frustrated and annoyed with the lack of recognition of their ability, but equally determined to prove themselves capable. One of her participants stated:

> Women still have to continually prove themselves worthy of status in the outdoors — they have to prove it to themselves and to others. I am still young and learning ... experience will give you confidence to believe in yourself. It's not enough to just be in a position of leadership, a woman has to justify that position. (p. 35-36)

Despite conventional and traditional notions that men are better outdoor leaders because of their strength and assumed leadership skills, findings in outdoor leadership effectiveness research show that women are performing well and in some cases, better than men (Neill, 1997; Phipps and Claxton, 1997). The study by Phipps and Claxton did not set out to measure gender difference. However, their findings showed that female instructors were ranked significantly higher than their male counterparts when scored by trained observers and activity participants. Notably, their study placed a high value on the interpersonal and group leadership skills required for instructor effectiveness. It placed less emphasis on strength and the technical skills that have historically been the measure of instructor effectiveness within the adventure recreation industry. It is encouraging that the skills for outdoor leaders are being researched and re-evaluated and that there is increasing recognition that good social and interpersonal skills are crucial to effective outdoor leadership. Perhaps some members of the adventure industry will now begin to move away from the description of interpersonal skills as "touchy, feely, girly shit". This statement, relating to the value of interpersonal skills, was made to a female instructor by an experienced male colleague during a staff training programme (Carter, 1998).

The self confidence of women working in the adventure industry field is strongly influenced by the attitude of others towards them. Levi (1991) gives an account of a year spent working at an outdoor centre in the United Kingdom. She entered her position as the female member of the centre's instructional team, somewhat inexperienced but well trained in outdoor and education skills. She found that her technical skills were ridiculed even though she held several national qualifications. She was often relegated to the tasks of driving the bus or doing maintenance. Levi states that she was verbally assaulted by a senior member of staff and given little support from the other male instructor as he believed in "learning the hard way" (p.7). She walked out of her position after a physical argument with the same senior member of staff who had previously verbally assaulted her. Her experience stripped her of self confidence. She did not return to outdoor education until some years later when she became part of a two year programme "Women in the Outdoors". It was only through involvement with that project that Levi found new confidence to work in outdoor education in schools again.

In my own current study, I interviewed a young woman, Jane, who had worked in adventure recreation since she was eighteen years of age. Her first full time working experience was similar in some ways to Levi's, though the level of harassment was much less. She was employed at an outdoor education centre owned by a private boy's school. She stated that she learnt "not to bite" when she was continually teased about her small stature and jokes were made about her perceived lack of strength. She stated that one of her male colleagues "really had a problem with women". If it was not for the support of other male staff, particularly the centre manager, she feels that she may not have coped with her first year of full time employment. Her primary method of coping was to remember that there were many things she could do that the guys could not, especially in relation to interpersonal skills. She retained her personal confidence, though not without recognising that it would be very easy to fall into a demoralising, submissive and accepting role.

Jane was not the only woman I spoke with who discussed the problem of retaining feelings of self confidence. TP worked in outdoor environments around the world as an archaeologist before developing an interest in working in adventure recreation. She initially worked as an archaeology specialist on eco-recreation tours. After extensive retraining, she now works as an outdoor educator in schools. Despite her years of diverse experience and training, she expressed a lack of confidence in her abilities. Much of that lack of confidence came from the lack of recognition she received from within the adventure recreation industry.

> You had to prove yourself first quite a lot before you would be
> accepted as any good and people were very reluctant to tell you that
> you were any good at things, they were much more prone to tell you

where your weaknesses lie, ... your self confidence gets a battering and mine definitely did. ... There are quite a few women in the outdoors who have been there for quite a while and now like (P) and she's only got her credibility because she's been there for so long. It's the time factor and I don't think the time factor is such a great thing for males, people tend to give them more credibility at the start. ... I mean I don't know, that's the truth, that's my general impression of it and I felt too that I wasn't given a lot of credit for past experience either. (Carter, 1998)

The assumption that women only gain credibility with the length of time they spend working in the outdoors speaks of the determination and perseverance of many of the women who are currently employed in adventure recreation. It is almost as if women must be tested to see if they have the necessary stamina to remain in the industry. Unfortunately they are tested on many levels. Not only must they learn to cope with sexist language and attitudes, they must learn to cope with being undervalued and underestimated for much of their working lives. One other woman I interviewed, Kosci, reported that she felt her position with one outdoor company was simply that of the "token female". She was rarely called upon to demonstrate her skills, despite the fact that she had several international qualifications and over five years of working experience. She believed that the company involved was simply propping up its corporate image. It wanted to be seen to be "doing the right thing" by employing a woman.

Discrimination against women in the workplace is not restricted to the adventure recreation industry. Smith and Hutchinson (1995) discuss gender issues across a wide variety of industries. What is important to recognise in the adventure recreation industry is the contradiction between philosophy and practice, the gap between hope and happening. The adventure recreation industry supposedly provides opportunities for all of its participants to develop self confidence through personal discovery, risk taking and challenge. If the primary aim of many adventure recreation and education programmes is to assist in the development of self esteem, why is it that so many of the women who work in the industry report that, for them, the opposite actually occurs? It is my belief that male defined models of achievement do little to recognise, let alone meet, the needs of women. The adventure industry itself, and particularly its women, must begin to insist on alternative models to the masculinist notions of adventure being adopted and recognised. Only when the adventure recreation industry bands together to break traditional stereotypes of adventure as masculine, will women gain credible employment within the industry.

Women sticking their foot in the (out)doors

Despite the recognised dominance of males in the adventure recreation industry, little by little the workplace is changing. In a recruitment drive in 1996, the Australian Outward Bound School received 170 applications. Fifty-four percent were from men, with the remaining forty-six per cent from women. Five women and four men were selected to train as instructors (Neill, 1997). The North American National Outdoor Leadership School has a goal of forty per cent of its staff positions filled by women, to match the percentage of female students. This is an honourable target, but one they are still to meet (Koesler, 1993). It is projected that more women than men will participate in backpacking and hiking by the year 2000 (Kelly, 1987, p. 46). In addition, the percentage of women participating in all aspects of adventure recreation is increasing faster than men (Henderson, 1992). With these predictions and trends, there is heightened recognition that it is important for outdoor programmes to incorporate a female perspective (Jordan, 1992; Knapp, 1985; Mitten, 1985, Warren and Rheingold, 1993).

One of the women interviewed for my study expressed the opinion that, at the moment, women seeking employment in adventure recreation held an advantage over males. This was primarily due to their scarcity. There were far fewer skilled women available to work in the industry than men. In addition, many commercial outdoor providers had recognised that they needed to employ instructors skilled in both technical and personal skills in order to offer a balanced product to their clients.

There is now sufficient research available that recognises the so called 'soft' (personal) skills as crucial to outdoor leadership, particularly in industry sectors that use adventure recreation activities to achieve therapeutic outcomes (Gass, 1993). Even though technical skills appear to be the most common measure of employability (Green, 1994), it is personal skills that are perceived by many people within the adventure recreation industry to be the most important skills in recruiting trainees in outdoor leadership. A study undertaken by Priest (1989) invited outdoor leadership experts from five countries (Australia, Canada, United Kingdom, New Zealand and the United States) to rank components important for an effective outdoor leader. The top three attributes identified as critical to outdoor leaders included judgement based on experience, awareness and empathy for others, and a flexible leadership style. This study suggested that it was important for outdoor leaders to have technical skills and safety skills, but that technical skills were not considered an important factor in assessing suitable trainees to enter the industry. Behaviour, philosophy and self concept were deemed to be more important at a novice level.

There is still a need to positively recognise the value of developing interpersonal skills in conjunction with technical skills, rather than valuing one set of skills more than the other. It is also important that the industry remove the gender assignment currently attached to these 'hard' and 'soft' skills. The development of technical skills is not the sole domain of males any more than interpersonal skills are the domain of women. In most sectors of the industry it is no longer appropriate for employment and promotion opportunities to be based on technical skill standards alone. If this more balanced direction continues and women are encouraged to remain within the industry, there is an expectation that opportunities will open up and women will take on more significant roles.

Where to from here?

The major problem identified in this paper is that, despite the recognition of the need for feminine perspectives in adventure programming, masculinist attitudes restrict employment opportunities for women. Most training is offered under traditionally masculine models and women are a significant minority at almost all levels of the industry. Instead of experiencing empower- ment through involvement in adventure recreation, many women feel oppres- sion in situations where men dominate (Humberstone, 1996). Recognition of these factors is one thing, how the industry goes about changing them is another. Several researchers have suggested ways in which some of the recog- nised problems for women may be alleviated, to assist them in developing, and retaining, feelings of self worth, value and confidence.

Knapp (1985) felt there was a need to develop more androgynous leaders, leaders who displayed masculine and feminine behavioural traits, as appropriate, rather than relying on traditional masculinist models of leader- ship. He proposed that staff training should include an awareness of gender issues and should place greater emphasis upon human relations skills. In addition, he identified the need to balance the number of qualified male and female leaders to serve as role models for participants of both sexes.

There has also been a call for the development of more women only train- ing courses in order for women to attain basic technical skills in supportive, non competitive environments (Johnston, 1990; Loeffler, 1995; Mitten, 1985). Johnson, in particular, felt it was important for women to learn to function independently of men. She felt that men tended to step in to help women and to want to remove the source of any fear or difficulty. It was perhaps this misplaced chivalry that kept women from truly exploring their own potential and developing confidence in their own ability. There is value in the idea of women learning with women. It is understood that, in general, women enter the outdoors with a different acculturation to men, and seek different outdoor experiences than men (Mitten, 1985). If women are given the opportunity to develop basic skills with other women, they may have more opportunity to realise their potential without the constant comparison to male defined standards. It is then more likely that they will develop a higher level of self confidence and a greater sense of personal identity, belonging and visibility.

Loeffler (1997) takes this idea one step further. Not only does she see a need for women only training, she also believes that women need to spend time in the outdoors on their own. It is only in this way that all external factors can be removed and women can gain true insight into their own level of ability. This proposal is based on her own experience. While instructing a wilderness course one summer, she was required to go out on reconnaissance for the next day's group hike. She was heading out alone and, despite hundreds of day of wilderness experience, she was doubtful of her ability to do the navigation required and to handle the terrain alone. Loeffler related how important it was for her to realise her own level of competence. She found the experience "exhilarating and empowering to be totally responsible for route finding, navigation and decision making" (p.121). It was through this experience that Loeffler was able to reassess her ability. She could not attribute her success to co-instructors or students. There was no one else to rely on. She was totally responsible for her success and could not deny her own level of competence.

It may not be possible for every woman who wants to work in adventure recreation to experience a solo expedition such as that undertaken by Loeffler. However, her story demonstrates how important it is for women, even those with years of outdoor experience, to find ways to assess their skills objectively. Women must learn to appreciate their own level of skill, to understand that they have many attributes that contribute to the adventure recreation industry. The industry needs to see through traditional male practices, to look beyond the stereotypes, to allow women to develop their own identity, their own ways of working and confidence in their ability. It is important that women recognise their strengths and resist the historical, societal brainwashing that continues to play a part in determining women's role in the outdoors.

Perhaps the crux of this argument is not gender, but really more the issue of recognising and appreciating difference. This point was raised by one of the participants in my study. I asked her about the skills that women contributed to the company where she worked. This was her reply:

> I'm not sure that women necessarily have any skills any more than guys because I've met guys [who] work for us [who] are hugely empathetic... [they] have got the skills that women are supposed to

have and I've met girls who just don't have those things, who are not empathetic, who are self centred, are not good at relating to people. I've seen girls be typical male roles and males be typical girl roles so I'm not sure that there is actually anything different related to gender but I do find that it's a nice, happy, fun, less competitive environment when there's lots of girls around but it's quite an empowering environment when the guys are around because they are always off doing something different whereas the girls just want to sit and chat (laughs) which is great but both of them are quite different environments, there's definitely a different vibe when there is all guys working on a programme and all girls working on a programme. (Carter, 1998)

Regardless of gender, the adventure recreation industry must acknowledge that all of us, women and men, contribute something of ourselves to our working environments. Our individual personalities, experiences and skills amalgamate to form the style of outdoor leadership we choose to display. There is no one philosophy or one method or practice that needs to dominate any other, all can coexist in synergistic relationships. For this to be possible, the industry needs to acknowledge that it currently operates under a paradigm of masculine control that is no longer appropriate. It excludes women and restricts them from reaching their full potential. The adventure recreation industry needs to make a choice. It can retain its masculinist traditions or it can adopt an open minded approach that enables each individual to value their own experience and their own unique way of working outdoors.

References

Bialeschki, M. D. (1992) 'We said "Why not?": A historical perspective on women's outdoor pursuits' *Journal of Physical Education, Recreation and Dance* Vol. 63, No. 2): pp. 52–55.

Carter, M. (1998) Discussions with women employed in adventure recreation in Western Australia. Unpublished research transcripts.

Gass, M A. (1993) *Adventure therapy: Therapeutic applications of adventure programming*. USA: Kendall Hunt.

Green, M. (1994) 'A study of some of the influences affecting the learning of tertiary women involved in outdoor education'. Unpublished paper, School of Education, Deakin University, Geelong, Victoria.

Hawes, R. Bachelard, M. and Schubert, M. (1998) 'Blokey forces still deter women', *The Weekend Australian*, June 13–14: p. 7.

Henderson, K. A. (1992) 'Breaking with tradition — women and outdoor pursuits', *Journal of Physical Education, Recreation and Dance* Vol. 63, No. 2: pp. 49–51.

Humberstone, B. (1996) 'Other voices, other meanings? Technique and philosophy for outdoor adventure. The case for women', *The Journal of Adventure Education and Outdoor Leadership* Vol. 13, No. 2: pp. 47–51.

Johnson, D. (1990) 'Women in the outdoors', *The Journal of Adventure Education and Outdoor Leadership* Vol. 7, No. 3: pp. 38–40.

Jordan, D. J. (1992) 'Effective leadership for girls and women in outdoor recreation', *Journal of Physical Education, Recreation and Dance* Vol. 63, No. 2: pp. 61–64.

Kelly, J. (1987) *Recreation trends: Towards the year 2000*. Champaign, IL: Management Learning Laboratories Ltd.

Knapp, C. (1985) 'Escaping the gender trap: The ultimate challenge for experiential educators', *Journal of Experiential Education* Vol. 8, No. 2: pp. 16–19.

Koesler, R. (1993) *Wilderness leadership: Forging a new understanding of gender relationships*. Report submitted to the National Outdoor Leadership School, Wyoming, USA.

Levi, J. (1991) 'Entering the outdoor education profession: A high risk activity for women?', *The Journal of Adventure Education and Outdoor Leadership* Vol. 8, No. 1: pp. 7–8.

Loeffler, T. A. (1995) *Factors that influence women's career development in outdoor leadership*. Unpublished doctoral dissertation, University of Minnesota, Minneapolis, MN.

Loeffler, T.A. (1997) 'Assisting women in developing a sense of competence in outdoor programs', *Journal of Experiential Education* Vol. 20, No. 3: pp. 119–123.

Miner, J. L. (1990) 'The creation of Outward Bound', in J. Miles and S. Priest (eds) *Adventure education*. State College, PA: Venture, pp. 55–66.

Mitten, D. (1985) 'A philosophical basis for a women's outdoor adventure program', *Journal of Experiential Education* Vol. 8, No. 2: pp. 20–24.

Neill, J T. (1997) 'Gender: How does it effect the outdoor education experience?', Conference paper presented at the 10th National Outdoor Education Conference, Collaroy Beach, New South Wales (January).

Phipps, M. L., and Claxton, D. B. (1997) 'An investigation into instructor effectiveness', *Journal of Experiential Education* Vol. 20, No. 1: pp. 40–46, 50.

Priest, S. (1989) 'International experts rank critical leadership concerns and components', *Journal of Physical Education, Recreation and Dance*, Vol. 60, No. 2: pp. 72–77.

Smith, C. and Hutchinson, J. (1995) *Gender: A strategic management issue.* Sydney: Business and Professional.

Stockham, K. (1996) 'Women, autobiography and mountaineering', Conference paper presented at the World Leisure and Recreation Association, 4th World Congress, Cardiff, UK (July).

Warren, K, and Rheingold, A. (1993) 'Feminist pedagogy and experiential education: A critical look', *Journal of Experiential Education* Vol. 16, No. 3: pp. 25–31.

Enhancing Self-esteem in Adolescent Girls: A Proposed Model for Adventure Education Programming

Karen L. Barak, Mary Anne Hedrich and Steven J. Albrechtsen

Department of Health, Physical Education, Recreation and Coaching, University of Wisconsin, Whitewater, USA

Adolescence is a critical time of change for youth. Visible changes to the physical body can be apparent during this time of life, yet important changes to emotional and social aspects of being may be less apparent. Attention has been specifically drawn to a virtually invisible change that occurs during adolescence through the work of the American Association of University Women (AAUW) in the early nineteen-nineties. Studies conducted by the AAUW revealed that self-esteem dropped for adolescent boys and girls. However, the drop in self-esteem levels was significantly greater for, and had more long term effects on adolescent girls and their lives (1991, 1992). These findings have been supported by the work of other researchers and writers such as Brown and Gilligan (1992), Hedrich (1993), Backes (1994), Orenstein (1994), and Pipher (1995).

The AAUW (1992: p. 23) defined self-esteem as individuals' "faith in themselves, their belief in their abilities and their confidence in their capabilities to live their dreams and determine their own future". Wright (1982) indicated that self-esteem is the way that we feel about ourselves. It is the worth that we assign to our self description. Wright believed that self-regard is an appropriate synonym for self-esteem. Battle (1990) wrote that self-esteem refers to the perception the individual possesses of her or his own worth ... it is the composite of feelings, hopes, fears, thoughts; views of what one is, what one has been, and what one might become. With these definitions in place, it is also important to note the caveat offered by Flansburg (1993: p. 4). "Although the term 'self-esteem' seems almost intuitively obvious, this is perhaps one of the reasons it is so difficult to define: its meaning is subject to many conscious and unconscious beliefs and values we hold about what is desirable and what is not". This statement serves to point out the complexities of the individual that can interact with the development of positive self-esteem.

It would seem difficult for adolescent girls to build positive self-esteem based on the dualistic messages they receive through cultural norms. These messages can be found in the media that suggest to girls they are only valued for a slim body image, sexual attractiveness, attentiveness to desires of others, or ability to raise a family. The result of these messages is to limit girls' ideals and future potentials. Other results might include the distressing differences found between responses to the questions 'what does it mean to be a boy?' and 'what does it mean to be a girl?'. While many characteristics associated with being a boy are generally viewed as positive and desirable, many of the characteristics associated with being a girl are viewed as negative or undesirable by both boys and girls (AAUW, 1991; Hedrich and Voss, 1995; Mee, 1995). Pipher believes these sorts of messages are devastating to adolescent girls' development of self (including self-esteem). Often adolescent girls develop 'false selves', a facade built to meet others' dualistic and unrealistic expectations of them as girls. The ideal situation would seem to be that boys and girls are valued equally for their potential contributions to humankind, whether those contributions be similar or different from one another.

It is apparent that there is room for the implementation of multiple strategies to enhance self-esteem of adolescent girls. There is a wide array of human potential development opportunities stemming from the various values of racial/ethnic, socio-economic, academic, geographic, and/or family groups; the social environment and; one's personal abilities, interests, and experiences. Strategies should consider influential experiences including sexism, racism, classism, ageism, ableism, or other individual situations. We propose that adventure education is one such strategy.

So how might adventure education contribute to the development of positive self-esteem? Adventure education may provide an activity where girls can identify the competencies and abilities they possess, along with their contributions to problem-solving and group processes. It is a programme which might provide the opportunity for adolescent girls to be true to themselves, to gain confidence in their abilities, and to explore issues of concern to them. An ideal programme of adventure education designed to enhance esteem in adolescent girls would break down stereotypical views of 'boys versus girls' behaviours; build confidence and self-esteem; and allow degrees of choice, control, and power. It would also provide role models and examples of androgynous behaviours, and address participant concerns, while fostering respect, care, and concern for programme participants and their individual circumstances.

An overview of adventure education

The term adventure education encompasses a variety of activities or experiences such as wilderness trekking, games, initiatives or performance of tasks on ropes suspended high above the ground. While these activities are diverse in nature, they are related by several key elements. These elements would include: 1) Learning, 2) Risk, and 3) Facilitation. To provide context for adventure education activities an overview of these elements is provided.

Learning

Typically learning from adventure education is gained by moving though the experiential learning cycle. Nadler and Luckner (1992) note that most all experiential learning models involve at least four steps including 1) the experience, 2) reflection, 3) processing, and 4) application. Experiential models depict a flow of events through which the learner may discover, strengthen, or clarify knowledge, values, or skills.

The experience phase of learning consists of the activity itself and all of its integral parts. It includes tasks, interaction with others, environment, and the individual. It includes feelings that may be experienced: frustration, triumph, discomfort, or joy. The reflection phase provides an opportunity for the individual learner to remember and identify the components of the experience which are significant to them. This is an individual task, and different individuals typically identify some similar and some different significant pieces of the experience. The processing phase allows for sharing individual reflections with others who were involved in the experience. During this phase the group facilitator may ask key questions to stimulate discussion. Processing allows group members to see that not everyone views the experience from the same frame of reference. It can allow individuals to consider the experience from a different point of view, or notice significant aspects of the experience they may have missed in their personal reflection. The application phase occurs when individuals formulate ways to apply concepts, ideas, skills, or values which they have identified through this process to situations in their individual lives.

Facilitators typically construct the activities to be experienced during the experience phase of the experiential learning cycle. In examining the idea of providing experiential education activities to women, Warren and Rheingold (1996) indicated that a constructed experience may be incompatible with feminist approaches because it ignores participants' past experiences. In contrast, one might consider that individual selves are sum totals of what is experienced and learned in the past. While individuals participate in a constructed experience, past experiences and perceptions of self are inherently present. These experiences, knowledges, and perceptions are part of the interpretation of experience, and are reflected as a valuable part of self in the processing and application phases of the experiential learning process. Constructed experiences may simply provide a basis for common discussion.

Feminist theory indicates that women's ways of knowing are based on connection and relationship. Through use of the experiential learning process in adventure education, it is possible to make and then discuss connections and relationships. When the importance of girls' observations and contributions are publicly affirmed through processing and application, a foundation for building self-worth and self-esteem is created.

Risk

Risk is the second related component in adventure education. Risk is associated with unknown or questionable outcomes and may be experienced as physical, psychological, and/or social risk. What constitutes risk is highly individual and personal. Physical risk may be perceived when one feels their physical being is in danger, such as from falling from a height. Psychological risk may be perceived when one faces a fear. There is a psychological risk in turning out the lights when one is afraid of the dark. Social risk may be perceived when one feels they are acting outside of their assigned or adopted roles, such as when a shy person demonstrates leadership skills to a group.

Some would prefer to call risk 'challenge' because the situation offers controlled danger that is minimal. Challenge suggests a more positive outlook on the activity or experience because individuals are free to a degree to determine the parameters of the challenge and to anticipate personally desired outcomes. Risk hints, possibly darkly, of the uncontrollable and the unknown. However, there are good risks and bad risks. Participants in adventure education may develop the skills to discern the difference between good and bad risks, and apply that discrimination in their real lives. Positive experiences with good risks encourage further positive risk-taking. When conducted appropriately, risk in adventure education is primarily perceptual in nature due to precautions and understanding possessed by facilitators of the adventure education experience.

Facilitation

Skilled facilitators are essential to a safe adventure education programme, and have the potential to make large contributions to the degree of learning which can occur during adventure education experiences. Facilitators must have an excellent understanding of group dynamics in order to stimulate observations and discussions without undue influence on the group. The facilitator is not 'telling' or 'lecturing' the group, but asking questions or encouraging conversation to assist the group to discover or reveal knowledge that individuals already possess through their experiences and observations. The facilitator must understand the risks inherent in specific activities and adequately prepare group members both physically and mentally to work through challenges. The facilitator must know safety techniques and limitations. It takes a skilled facilitator to monitor all aspects of individual perception of risk.

These three elements, Learning, Risk, and Facilitation combine to create similarities between all adventure education experiences. A Mind Map Model of adventure education has been created to conceptualize considerations in adventure education for developing self-esteem in adolescent girls. The mind map technique depicts ideas and the connections between ideas as they develop. In building this model, Learning, Risk and Facilitation have been incorporated into a single basic unit to indicate the inherent parts of adventure education experiences. Also inherent to the adventure education experience are the participants themselves, in this case adolescent girls. There are also differences among various adventure education activities which might be considered in developing a design for the purposes of enhancing self-esteem of adolescent girls. These differences are depicted in the model as three broad categories including 1) Accessibility, 2) Facilitator training and technique, and 3) Outcomes. These three categories will be expanded in the following sections. The beginnings of a Mind Map Model of adventure education which depict the experience and the three categories can be seen in Figure 1.

Accessibility

If adventure education experiences can enhance self-esteem, it is desirable to allow as many girls as possible to participate. Accessibility can make a difference in who and how individuals will participate. In programme design, this may mean examining elements such as timing, equipment, and location, which tie together to heavily influence the cost of the activity. In considering these elements, connections can be made between other components. The mind map model is expanded in Figure 2 to include the concepts of timing, equipment, and location linked to costs, and their further connections.

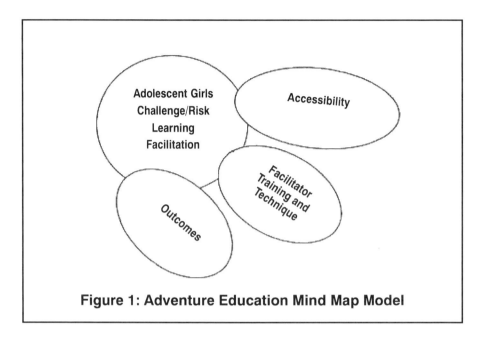

Figure 1: Adventure Education Mind Map Model

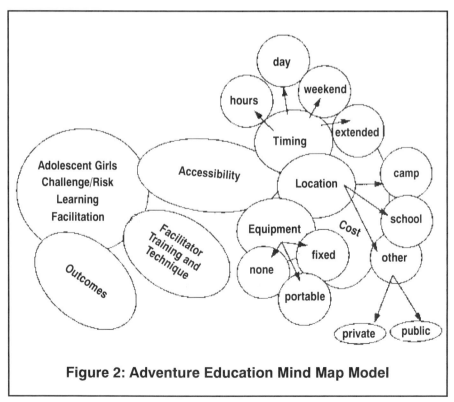

Figure 2: Adventure Education Mind Map Model

Timing

adventure education might be conducted in a variety of time schematics. Short periods of time scheduled in a series may best meet the needs of girls who perceive simply participating in adventure education as a challenge. Others may benefit from day long, weekend, or extended period of time outings. For instance, a wilderness excursion cannot be conducted in a one hour time block, which might be the amount of time available for adventure education if offered through a physical education course in schools. Or, if activities are split into a series of meetings, it may be possible to have participants reflect in journals, as opposed to using 'scheduled' activity time for the reflection phase of the experiential learning cycle. Timing can be directly related to the location of the adventure education experience.

Location

The wilderness may be the first image to come to mind when thinking of adventure education experiences. Connection between nature, humanity, spirituality and feminism as related to the natural environment has been noted by Henderson (1996), and might therefore provide an excellent opportunity for building self-esteem for adolescent girls. However, while an outdoor setting may be desirable for the aims of adventure education, it is not necessarily a requirement. Excursions which take girls into the wilderness as a unique environment have much to offer, however they may offer more challenge than younger, urban, or racially diverse adolescent girls find desirable. If challenge is not desirable, it will not be engaged with. Girls will not access undesirable experiences.

Leisure patterns and preferences of families are likely to effect involvements of adolescent girls in adventure education experiences. In fact, the AAUW (1991, 1992) found that families are more influential on adolescent girls than either their peers or teachers. Studies of patterns and preferences of leisure activities have shown that people in rural areas are more likely to have patterns of and preferences for outdoor activity, whereas people from urban areas are much more likely to have patterns of and preferences for indoor experiences. This appears to be a matter of exposure (or lack of exposure) and convenience. Games, initiatives, or portable elements can be offered in urban or rural areas, providing a wider range of accessibility to a variety of girls. Accessibility to the adventure education experience should be paramount in programme design, with the hope that initial experience may lead to a higher level of involvement for adolescent girls.

The provider of adventure education possesses a strong influence on both timing and location. If schools provide adventure education as part of the school curriculum in short blocks of time on an ongoing basis it is likely to be accessible to the greatest number of girls. If camps provide adventure education experiences, a wilderness location and a single longer block of time becomes more accessible. Community agencies, public and private, may have access to a combination of sites and scheduling options and are thereby able to implement adventure education in multiple locations, with various timing combinations. Collaboration between multiple providers may provide the resources required to attain the greatest design flexibility and lowest cost possible.

Equipment

Equipment makes adventure education an intriguing programme for participants. Unique props and an unfamiliar environment can set the stage for growth and learning for individuals. When unusual items are used there is a lack of expectations for who might control or use equipment or objects based on gender stereotypes or past use. Thus, girls have the opportunity to explore behaviours beyond gender role expectations without being chastised or sanctioned through social norms.

As greater numbers of people participate in adventure education experiences, it is likely they will discuss the activity with friends, classmates, and family, where some expectations will be developed. If participants enter a programme with preconceived notions about how to solve a presented problem, it can serve to de-rail the processes involved in adventure education. The implication for adventure education is that there must be a wide variety of experiences used, and that the development and re-creation of equipment, stories, scenarios, and frames for experiences must be continual. Creativity and novelty must be infused into experiences to keep programmes fresh and continually challenging.

The types of equipment necessary for specific activities influences the location, and thus the accessibility of adventure education experiences. Required equipment may be minimal for games to acquaint participants with each other, to practice spotting for another person undertaking a challenging activity or to develop other skills which can be used in later activities, or for low element experiences. If portable equipment can be used accessibility is increased. Arranging for games and initiatives which require fewer props and less equipment would also increase accessibility to adventure education.

Cost

Expense of adventure education has been noted as a barrier for both agency providers and participants (Warren, 1985; Ocker *et al.*, 1997). Designing programmes for accessibility based on cost does effect programme offerings in terms of programme design. Less extensive programmes, creative equipment, and public offerings of adventure education may assist with increasing access to adventure education experiences.

Facilitator training and technique

Training is typically provided to those who facilitate adventure education experiences. However, the content of the training component, even if focused on expected topics such as group dynamics and safety, has the potential to vary greatly. The following considerations, type and/or degree of risk, degree of choice, and societal and girls' self-esteem issues, are appropriate to examine in developing a programme of adventure education designed to enhance self-esteem of adolescent girls. These considerations do not constitute a full training programme. Instead, they reflect additional considerations to be included in an already developed facilitator training programme. The Mind Map Model is expanded in Figure 3 to depict these issues and their connections.

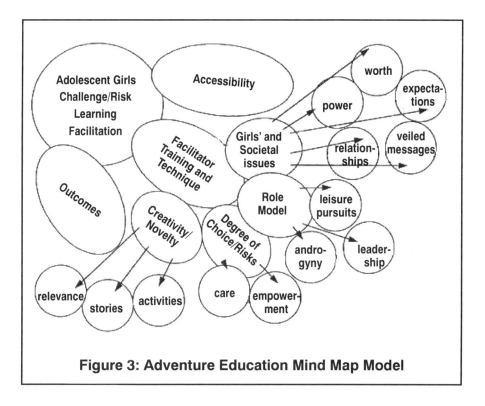

Figure 3: Adventure Education Mind Map Model

Girls' and societal self-esteem issues

Research on self-esteem in adolescent girls and research on outdoor/ experiential learning has pointed to the importance of facilitators who can serve as role models for participants (Emil, 1997; Hutton 1993; Mee 1995; Morse, 1997; Rothenburg, 1995; Roberts and Henderson, 1997; Sautzyk and Poorman, 1994; Warren, 1985). In several cases participants in self-esteem situations or outdoor experiences expressed a desire for leaders who could role model desirable behaviour. Many girls and women are likely to become interested or more involved with activities if the facilitator possesses characteristics with which they can identify, such as racial/ethnic background, gender, ability level, or other attributes.

In several school settings where group programmes were developed to enhance self esteem, it was found that one of the greatest needs was to create an awareness of women's issues with faculty and staff. Pipher (1995) points out the importance of heightening girls' awareness of inconsistent messages about women's worth communicated through society. By making this a priority of an adventure education programme, issues of power and oppression, of contradicting messages related to appropriate roles, body images, or use of oppressive language can be unveiled. Awareness of these contradictions can assist girls' understanding of why they may feel internal conflicts in relation to their self worth. In order to expose these issues, facilitators must have an understanding of them. A recommended component of facilitator training relates to developing an understanding of such women's issues.

There are many things that facilitators might model in order to communicate the worth, value, and respect for adolescent girls. Mitten (1996) indicated that facilitators may operate out of an 'ethic of caring' which is consistent with developmental patterns of girls as indicated by the work of Gilligan (1982). Facilitators who can understand and operate from this level may be more effective at enhancing self-esteem of girls, and encouraging them to be true to themselves.

Henderson and Bialeschski (1987), and Pate (1994) indicated that studies show people who demonstrate androgynous behaviours may be better able to adapt to everyday living situations, and are generally better adjusted to coping with situations that may occur as part of everyday life. If facilitators are able to role model androgynous behaviours it can serve to indicate that individuals are not required to adhere to the stereotypical roles outlined by societal messages.

Degree of choice and risk

An issue central to feminist theory is dealing with the power imbalance between the oppressed and oppressor in society (Henderson, 1997; Mitten, 1996; Morse, 1997). The concern extends to the desire for equitable sharing of power between individuals so that all may be respected and valued. In society, those with lesser power also possess fewer opportunities to choose for themselves because the oppressor makes decisions and choices for the oppressed. Choice is an issue that is related to power. Adventure education has the opportunity to offer 'challenge by choice'. This means that participants can share power by being allowed to choose whether or not they wish to participate in the challenge. Girls may experience the opportunity to make choices through adventure education. Facilitators must understand the roots of power imbalance, and structure experiences to illuminate issues of power.

Activities that are selected for adventure education experiences by their nature can offer greater or lesser amounts of choice. Issues of safety must be balanced with choice. For instance, if the adventure experience involves rugged back county travel, the choice to participate can be made at the beginning of the trip. However, once the group is out in the wilderness, it is not practical for individuals to decide they will no longer participate. For safety reasons they cannot be left in the middle of rugged terrain while the rest of the group pushes onward!

Different activities provide various risks or challenges to participants. Activities are chosen based on goals for the participant group. Building group connections is a primary consideration in adventure education designed to enhance self-esteem. Pipher (1995) discusses the scapegoating of girls by other girls, and the difficulty that it produces. If issues can be processed within a trusted group, girls can emerge with healthier senses of self-esteem and respect for others. Establishing connections can build a powerful support system between adolescent girls. Concerns for developing relationships point toward offering adventure education experiences such as games, problem solving initiatives and low-level ropes course activities which rely on group participation and processing. Experiences designed to allow participants to bond may offer social challenges to participants. Such activities set the stage for building trust, and further communication. In contrast, performance of tasks on ropes suspended high above the ground can provide individual challenges without a strong interaction between group members in solving the challenge. These activities offer higher degrees of perceived physical and psychological challenge. For older adolescent girls, who are beginning to establish their identity separate from their families, these activities become more appropriate as an integrative piece of the programme design. For younger adolescent girls, this individualized challenge structure is not a primary concern.

Finally, as previously mentioned in the equipment subsection of this chapter, creativity and novelty must be continually infused into experiences to keep programmes fresh and challenging. Facilitators should/must be aware of their role in modifying and developing experiences for this reason.

Outcomes

Self-esteem has been the focal outcome for this description of adventure education experience. However, complexity in the development of self and the wide range of potential benefits make considering other outcomes a constructive process. The Mind Map Model does not include all of the potential benefits of adventure education. However, in addition to the benefit of enhanced self-esteem, the Mind Map Model includes the following: developing personal values, self-insight, knowledge, skills, and leisure pursuits; enhancing communication, problem solving and critical thinking abilities; experiencing the freedom to explore, availability of androgynous roles, and physical safety; learning to be true to one's self; unveiling dualistic message about women; recognizing the worth of girls and; gaining competency. In the process of considering how to develop a meaningful conceptualization of outcomes several arrangements might be considered.

One way to conceptualize outcomes would be to connect the potential benefits through the categories of 'Knowledge', 'skills', and 'Abilities' as depicted in Figure 4a. These categories are often used in professional hiring practices to develop a list of attributes that are important for potential candidates. However, if potential outcomes are grouped in this way, there is room for confusion as to where the outcomes might be placed that are related to character development or behaviours which allow one to explore new roles. While this scheme is often useful, it is not the only potential way to arrange outcomes.

Another arrangement that could be used would connect outcomes through the categories of 'Mind', 'spirit', and 'Body' as depicted in Figure 4b. However, in connecting potential outcomes through these categories, confusion occurs as to which outcome relates to which specific classification. Some outcomes distinctly show relationships to more than one of the identified categories. Arrows might be used to show relationships between multiple categories, but perhaps there are more helpful ways to arrange potential outcomes.

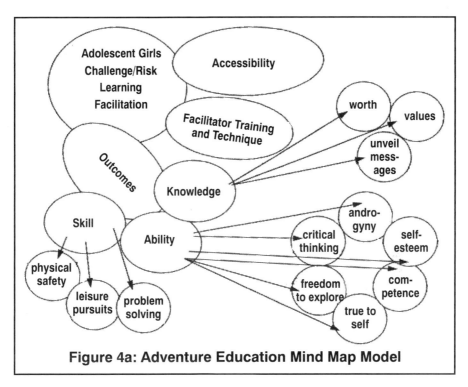

Figure 4a: Adventure Education Mind Map Model

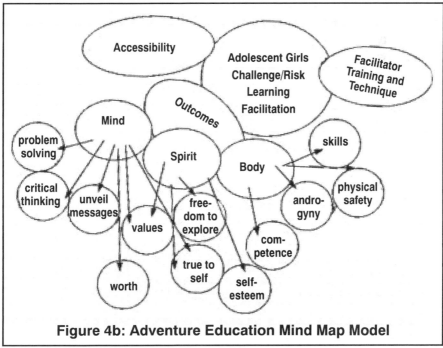

Figure 4b: Adventure Education Mind Map Model

Another way to conceptualize potential outcomes is by developing connections through categories which arose from qualitative research conducted by Barak (1995) while examining college freshmen and adventure education. These categories included 'Self-insight', 'Communication', and 'Problem-solving' as depicted in Figure 4c. But, once again these classifications may not provide clear cut boundaries within which to place adventure education outcomes.

Since in this case adventure education focuses on developing self-esteem, self-esteem might be considered to be the single category of benefits that are available through adventure education. In the case of designing adventure education programmes to enhance self-esteem in adolescent girls, this seems to be a reasonable arrangement for examining outcomes. This conceptualization is depicted by Figure 5.

Finally, classification of outcomes of this model might simply be designed without emphasis on grouping outcomes, but simply provide a perspective on the variety of outcomes which might be obtainable through a programme of adventure education. This conceptualization can be seen in Figure 6.

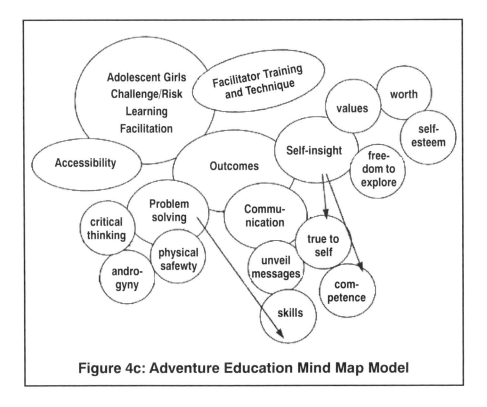

Figure 4c: Adventure Education Mind Map Model

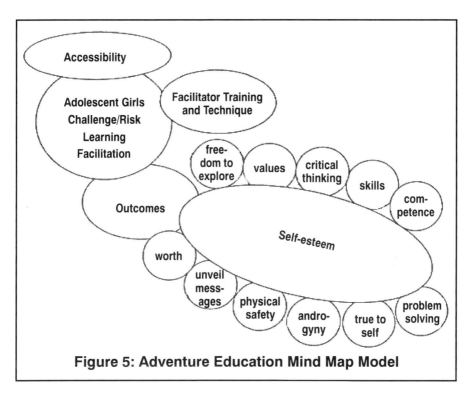

Figure 5: Adventure Education Mind Map Model

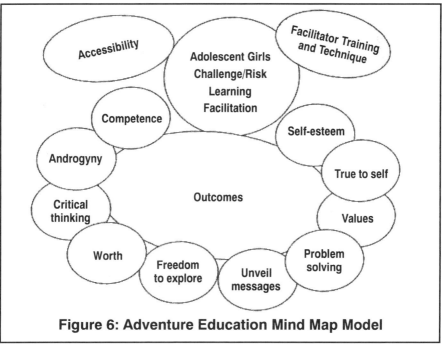

Figure 6: Adventure Education Mind Map Model

Summary

There is an established need for enhancing self-esteem in adolescent girls. Adventure education experiences include components that might effectively encourage the development of self-esteem. Adventure education experiences should be modified specifically for the purpose of enhancing self-esteem in adolescent girls by giving consideration to facilitator selection, training and skills development; accessibility and acceptability of programme to participants; issues that are specific to girls and women; anticipated desired outcomes and other potential outcomes; adolescent developmental stages and patterns; the social environment of the participants; and location, timing, equipment, and costs involved with the activity. The Mind Map Model provides a way to consider elements of adventure education, and concepts of importance when dealing with the goal of enhancing self-esteem in adolescent girls.

There is still more work to do in this area. A greater awareness of the usefulness of adventure education in increasing self-esteem in adolescent girls might allow more girls to participate in such activities. Adventure education might be incorporated into activities and experiences offered by various societal institutions concerned with young women and youth in general. A collection of works related to adventure education and the development of self-esteem would be a helpful resource for those concerned with these issues. Additionally, continued research on enhancing self-esteem and other benefits, and the expansion of the Mind Map Model can provide rich areas for additional research. This work might produce better measures by which to evaluate specific adventure education experiences.

References

Association of University Women (AAUW) (1991) *Shortchanging girls, shortchanging America. A nationwide poll to assess self-esteem, educational experiences, interest in math and science, and career aspirations of girls and boys ages 9–15.* Washington, DC: Author. ED 340657

American Association of University Women (AAUW) (1992) *Shortchanging girls, shortchanging America: A call to action.* Annapolis Junction, MD: Author. ED 340658.

Backes, J. (1994) 'Bridging the gender gap: Self-concept in the middle grades', Schools in the Middle Vol. 3, No. 3: pp. 19–23. EJ 483319.

Barak, K. (1995) 'Adventure education and college student development: An exploratory study', Ann Arbor, MI: UMI Microfilm 9536795.

Battle, J. (1990) *9 to 19: Crucial years for self-esteem in children and youth.* Seattle, Wash. : Special Child Publications.

Brown, M. Gilligan C. (1992) *Meeting at the crossroads: Women's psychology and girls' development.* Cambridge, MA: Harvard University Press.

Emil, C. (1993) *Strengthening the self-esteem of adolescent girls within the public school systems.* ED 375346.

Flansburg, S. (1993) *Building self: Adolescent girls and self-esteem working paper 2.* Newton, MA: Women's Educational Equity Act Publishing Center. ED 371250.

Gilligan, C. (1982) *In a different voice: Psychological theory and women's development.* Cambridge, PA: Harvard University Press.

Hedrich, M.A. (1993) 'Promoting relevance, self-esteem, and reasonable causal attribution in health education: Cardiopulmonary resuscitation as a strategy'. Ph.D. thesis. Madison, WI: University of Wisconsin-Madison.

Hedrich, M.A. and Voss, R. (1996) 'Ninth graders' views about the opposite sex and themselves', *Journal of Family and Consumer Sciences* (Fall): pp. 9–12.

Henderson, K. (1996) 'Women and the outdoors: Toward spiritual empowerment', in K. Warren (ed) *Women's voices in experiential education.* Dubuque, IA: Kendall/Hunt Publishing Company, pp. 193–202.

Henderson, K. (1997) 'Ecofeminism and experiential education', *Journal of Experiential Education* Vol. 20, No. 3: pp. 130-133.

Henderson, K. and Bialeschski, D. (1987). 'Viva la differencia!', *Camping Magazine* (February), Martinsville, IN: American Camping Association: pp. 20–22.

Hutton, S. (1993) *Enabling visions: Self-esteem of junior high girls.* ED 364 789.

Mee, C. (1995) *Middle school voices on gender identity.* Washington, DC: Office of Educational Research and Improvement.

Mitten, D. (1996) 'The value of feminine ethics in experiential education teaching and leadership', in K. Warren (ed) *Women's voices in experiential education.* Dubuque, IA: Kendall/Hunt Publishing Company, pp. 159–171.

Morse, A. (1997) 'Gender conflict in adventure education: Three feminist perspectives', *Journal of Experiential Education* Vol. 20, No. 3: pp. 124–129.

Nadler, R.S. and Luckner, J.L. (1992) *Processing the adventure experience: Theory and practice.* Dubuque, IA: Kendall/Hunt Publishing Company.

Ocker, J., Schmitt, S. and Vance, S. (1997) 'A survey of the use of adventure programming in new student orientation', *Proceedings of the National Conference on Undergraduate Research.* Austin, TX: National Council for Undergraduate Research.

Orenstein, P. (1994) *Schoolgirls: Young women, self-esteem, and the confidence gap.* New York: Doubleday.

Pate, L. (1997) 'Research update: Adolescent sex-role stereotyping: Change through wilderness courses', *Journal of Experiential Education* Vol. 20, No. 3: pp. 161–165.

Pipher, M. (1995) *Reviving Ophelia: Saving the selves of adolescent girls.* New York: Ballentine Books.

Roberts, N. and Henderson, K. (1997) 'Women of color in the outdoors: Culture and meanings', *Journal of Experiential Education* Vol. 20, No. 3: pp. 134–142.

Rothenburg, D. (1995) 'Supporting girls in early adolescence', *Eric Digest,* Urbana, IL: Clearinghouse on Elementary and Early Childhood Education.

Sautzyk, A. and Poorman, M. (1994) *Transition to adolescence program: A program to empower early adolescent girls.* San Diego, CA: Society for Research on Adolescence. ED 370 062 8.

Warren, K. and Rheingold, A. (1996) 'Feminist pedagogy and experiential education: A critical look', in K. Warren (ed) *Women's voices in experiential education.* Dubuque, IA: Kendall/Hunt Publishing Company: pp. 118–129.

Warren, K. (1985) 'Women's outdoor adventures: Myth and reality', *Journal of Experiential Education* Vol. 8, No. 2: Boulder, CO: Association for Experiential Education: pp. 10–14.

Wright, A. (1982) 'The effects of high adventure activities on adolescent self-concept: A comparison of situationally specific self concept measurements and global self-concept measurements', Paper presented at the National Convention of the American Camping Association. ED 224 791

Gendered 'Natural' Spaces: a Comparison of Contemporary Women's Experiences of Outdoor Adventure (UK) and Friluftsliv (Norway)

Barbara Humberstone
Buckinghamshire Chilterns University College, UK

Kirsti Pedersen
Finnmark College, Alta, Norway

This paper presents part of an ongoing exploration of the practice and ideology of friluftsliv[1] and outdoor adventure education/nature-based sport in Norway and the UK. Our overall interest is the creation of conceptual bases upon which further comparative research can be developed. Our concern is to develop an approach that is sensitive to the differences and contradictions within and between the various 'cultures' of outdoor adventure and friluftsliv and which is also sensitive to the social and cultural changes in post-modern society which shape gender identities, structures and relationship. We raise questions about the contradictions and changes in these cultures and explore how they may be interpreted and conceptualised theoretically. The methodological approach chosen here in this paper is a brief comparative review of current sociological research on gender/women and outdoor adventure in UK and friluftsliv in Norway.

'Nature' and 'culture'

As Raymond Williams (1976; 1988) and others point out, both terms 'nature' and 'culture' are notoriously difficult to define. Since this project is concerned to explore the different cultures of outdoor adventure (nature-based sport) in UK and friluftsliv (open air life/life in nature) in Norway from feminist perspectives, it is evident that the way in which these cultures are implicated and embedded in notions and ideologies of 'nature' is indeed complex. The complexities of culture in respect of such activities in nature are highlighted in Humberstone *et al.* (1998) and Pedersen (1993a; 1995; 1998a, 1998b). Whilst Humberstone (1998) touches upon the contradictions and ambiguities of the concept nature, its use and abuse as ideological metaphor, for sports feminism and for nature-based sport (see also Allwood *et al.*, 1983). Pederson (1998b) focuses on the cultural diversities and contradictions occurring in outdoor recreation in a local society in Northern Norway that has undergone a rapid modernisation during the 1990s. Suffice it, for the purposes of this paper, for us to point to our critical re-reading of different forms of outdoor cultures. This critical re-reading is informed by contemporary re-conceptualisations of culture that has emerged from a variety of perspectives, not least contemporary feminisms. Consequently, outdoor cultures can no longer be taken to be merely a set of shared values and beliefs, taken-for-granted assumptions and ways of acting, but also it constitutes the ways in which such phenomena are constructed through systems of meanings, by webs of power and through the organisations and institutions that produce and legitimate them. Thus outdoor cultures, which themselves are creations of specific 'elective communities' (Weeks, 1993), are made up of the processes, knowledges and categories that are understood to constitute them. We therefore argue that different communities or cultures of outdoor adventure/ nature-based sport and friluftsliv will have similarities in their philosophies, categorisations and technologies (modes of proceeding and practices), but also there will be significant diversity. It is the sameness and diversity between these outdoor cultures both within and between our two nations that are our interest.

Historical and geographical contexts

The historical and physical geographical conditions which shape and have shaped the developments of the outdoor adventure in UK and friluftsliv in Norway are diverse and clearly have implications for our analyses. In examining these cultures, their gendered developments need to be located within historical and geographical contexts. Whilst Pedersen (1997) explores the embeddedness of masculinity in traditions of friluftsliv, we show elsewhere the historical interconnections of outdoor adventure and friluftsliv and the ways in which these cultures have been influenced both by the Romantic movements, by nationalistic ideology and the British male aristocracy, also acknowledging that these influences are shaped by landscapes and concepts of 'wilderness' that are frequently very different (Humberstone and Pedersen, forthcoming).

Women's experiences

Here, however, we focus on the women today and briefly examine aspects of current women's experiences of/in outdoor adventure in UK and friluftsliv in Norway.

Familial relations

One main focus of research on gender/women and outdoor adventure and friluftsliv is the ways in which patriarchal relations and traditional family life affect and influence women (Hage, 1988; Pedersen, 1992; 1994). Tradition-ally, socialisation in families and schools has tended to stimulate boys' interest in outdoor activities and sports more than girls'. Pedersen (1992) argues that the consideration to realise an active friluftsliv for one's own pleasure is a far greater organising principle in men's lives than in women's lives. In general men spend more time on friluftsliv and more often take part in weekend hikes and trips with other males that often last several days. On the other hand, women more often exercise friluftsliv with her family in the local environment. Thus friluftsliv might be interpreted as a social and cultural 'room of their own' for men and men's culture in the Norwegian culture and everyday life (Pedersen, 1993a). The preconditions for this, as for men's and children's free time more widely, is, however, the invisible and traditional work that women do in the family. This largely creates men's possibilities for friluftsliv, whilst reducing those of women's (Pedersen, 1992, 1997). Thompson (1997) shows a similar relationship in her study of Australia women's involvement in sport.

Likewise in the UK, women are frequently restricted in their outdoor adventure experiences as a consequence of their familial relations (see also Woodward, this volume). This was evident for many of the urban youth workers who attended women-only residential outdoor education programmes in Wales. Many had considerable difficulty in negotiating time away from their families. Nevertheless, this particular experience was a liberating turning point for one woman who, finding confidence whilst 'being away from the domestic environment', rejected those arrangement and later set forth to gain educational qualifications (see Humberstone and Collins, 1998). Notwith-standing, biographical research in the UK has also suggested that many women who have embarked on a 'career' in outdoor adventure education gained their first experiences in the outdoors either through their families or later were encouraged by men to take part in outdoor adventure activities (Allin, 1998; and this volume).

Establishing 'natural spaces of her own'; processes of breaking traditions and empowering women

In the late 1980s and in the beginning of the 1990s there has been a growth in female only groups exploring and enjoying the Antarctica, the Arctic, the Himalayas and Greenland as well as their own local natural spaces. There has also been a growth in woman-only nature-based sport or educational programmes (Warren, 1996; Humberstone and Collins, 1998; Humberstone and Lynch, 1992; Pedersen, 1993b, 1994). The former groups of women are well trained for specific expeditions that require technical competence at a high level, while the latter may be participants in a mass cultural movement of women into nature for pleasure and enjoyment or women involved in educational cultures for personal development. These last two sets of women do not necessarily need a high level of technical skill acquisition. However, they do require, even in the UK countryside, certain self sufficient safety skills, the learning of which frequently enhances women's self confidence and esteem (Humberstone, 1986; Humberstone and Collins, 1998). Like the women-only expeditions and educational programmes, women-only organisations such as the Wilderness Women, Woodswomen,(USA), å Åsgårdsreien, Inga Låmi (Norway) are breaking cultural barriers both on an individual and a cultural level as they also show that women's achievements and actions are not biologically (pre-)determined by their sex or genes. Indeed women's individual and collective actions and their overt independence challenge traditional concepts of what constitutes women's behaviours and abilities. This is exemplified by the changes in the ways in which women climbers have been represented and reported in the climbing press in the UK during the last 20 years. The front cover of *Climber* Journal, June 1998, has a strong image of a woman climber, Jo Maclaren, leading Fools Gold (E1, 6a) with 'head line', 'Girl Power, The rise and rise of women climbers: Louise Thomas in the Karakorum'. In the same edition, Douglas's (1998: p. 38) report on women climbers' perception of the international meet for women climbers held in Wales in May 1998 points to women's changing perceptions of their abilities and the 'huge improvements both in the standards of women climbing and in their numbers'. He asserts that partly as a consequence of changes in society, and despite women having to put up with some, 'unpleasant gossip', women-only climbing events had a significant influence on women climber's changes of perceptions and on male climber's understandings of women's abilities. The women themselves see these women -only events not as ends in themselves but ways of, 'seeing where we've got to and what we still need' (Celia Bull, cited in Douglas, 1998: p. 38).

Discussion

Women in outdoor adventure and friluftsliv may perform activities that may have been judged as 'unnatural' for the female body. This may also demonstrate an independent female identity and a strong female physic(ality). These women thus challenge the common cultural understandings of what it is possible and 'natural' for the female body to do. Most important is perhaps that these women challenge a masculine identity built upon the popular image of 'mastering' the wilderness. Thus they de-masculinize and de-mythologize the 'wilderness' as hard, tough etc. — as a 'natural' space that requires the utmost of male strength, endurance and courage. At the same time they break down the image of the dependent women who need men's protection (Pedersen, 1993b). However, to do this, women need not necessarily approach the Antarctica or other inaccessible areas and peaks. It can happen for young women, on occasions, in certain circumstances, with particular teaching approaches as part of a mixed-sex residential adventure experiences (Humberstone, 1986). As some women are creating a 'natural space of their own', they are at the same time breaking the boundaries of the private sphere. Thus they expand their range of acting and moving, and in so doing they challenge the traditional gender pre-assumptions, making other options visible. In some cases these actions mean that men are entering the private sphere to take over the everyday obligations in the household. However, other women, generally mothers or female friends, frequently take over these obligations in the private sphere when women enjoy themselves through outdoor adventure and friluftsliv (Pedersen, 1998b; Humberstone and Collins, 1998).

Research suggests that for some women the importance of establishing an individual 'room of their own' -to escape everyday life obligations-is the most important. Others are conscious about how their actions might be valuable for the expansion of cultural and geographical space for 'females and female culture' more generally. In addition women struggle to influence the public spheres of outdoor adventure/friluftsliv through gaining space and recognition in the media, influence in outdoor adventure organisations, in the school system and in research (see Humberstone, 1996; Pedersen 1993b; Pedersen 1998c).

Today reactions such as public ridicule and open exclusions which the 'female pioneers' faced (Ryall, 1985) are less frequent. Other reactions can, however, be seen; such as responses that try to devalue the achievements of women in various ways, or simply by not telling about them. In research there is a tendency not to include or relate to feminist critiques that are developing. There is also a tendency to re-formulate the male dominated history, and to co-opt women, as the perspective of the 'universalised man' which is interpreted as if it includes both women's and men's perspectives and experiences. This is exemplified in the editorial of the June editorial of *Climber* that comments on its focus on women, 'I have a pat saying. There is no such thing as women climbers... [they] are part of the norm' (p. 3).

Thus women who are breaking boundaries may have been highly appreciated and valued but also criticised as in popular media's responses to the death of Alison Hargreaves in the Himalayas in 1995. In this respect, what is happening in outdoor adventure and friluftsliv is an echo of what has happened in the rest of society. The mixed responses mirror the variations and contradictions in today's views about the place and significance of the women in outdoor adventure/friluftsliv specifically, and in society more generally. Humberstone (1998a: p. 387) argues "... that nature-based sports can not only reaffirm hegemonic masculinities ... but also, in certain conditions, transform how both masculine bodies and feminine are defined, which may 'benefit' nature"; while Pedersen (1994, 1998a) assumes that 'wilderness' can be a space for reaffirmation of hegemonic masculinities, but also a space for transforming a dominant understanding of what it is possible for women to do.

Paradoxically, a women-only approach is a two edged sword. If this strategy is cultivated and interpreted as the main or only strategy for change (not tied to specific historical situations), there is a danger that it will contribute to the reproduction of dichotomised gendered ways of thinking, and thereby 'ghettoise' women. This may reinforce and sustain a hierarchical structure that places woman in an underprivileged position compared to the universalised man (Humberstone 1998c). On the other hand, women-only contexts have the potential to empower women and to challenge women's perceptions of themselves (Humberstone, 1998b; Pedersen, 1993b). However, women may need to reflect upon how they want to use their newly developed strengths and competences.

Self-fulfilment, solidarity and global challenges

The notion and ideology that has symbolised the liberal feminist movement, characterised by women's striving to expand their possibilities as females within capitalist and patriarchal relations needs to be critically addressed within outdoor adventure/friluftsliv cultures, together with the romantic and naive understanding of 'the female culture' as essentially environmentally good (Humberstone 1998a). From a global perspective the question about women's rights to and possibilities for recreation, pleasure, challenge, self-fulfilment, and as a way of transcending the split between nature and culture that is a consequence of modernity, through outdoor adventure and friluftsliv as a phenomenon of surplus energy, may seem to be a luxury. This is something that is not within the reach of most women who live in non-industrialised countries or urban working class women in our own societies (Pedersen, 1998b), nor even most Black and Asian Britains (see Humberstone, 1999). For many women in non-industrialised countries their relationship to nature is connected to everyday work for a living. When the Women's Research Institute of the United Nation focus on women and sustainable development, they are concerned with water supply, health, energy, waste disposal, the effects of the use of fertilizers and pesticides, nuclear vaste etc. — not adventure and leisure (see Braidotti, Charkiewicz, Häusler and Wieringa, 1994; Salleh, 1997). This reminds us of the socio-cultural context, the 'situated-ness' and limitations of our analyses. It also reminds us of the necessity to develop solidarity with women who live in other geographical and socio-cultural 'spaces', and to establish a global perspective when we discuss and practice outdoor adventure and friluftsliv on 'our own terms' as visitors in 'remote' and 'wilderness' areas. Urban people's needs for sport and outdoor adventure in 'wild spaces' increase all over the world, and the colonisation of open spaces by sport continue (for example by the establishment of new areas for alpine skiing, golf etc.) (cf. Price, 1996; Eder, 1995). To be related to and dependent on the 'natural' environment out of necessity is something quite different from being related to nature and to experience closeness and oneness with nature during one's spare time (Pedersen 1998b).

Concluding remarks

While progress was one of the key words during the 19 th and 20 th century when outdoor adventure and friluftsliv developed, key concepts at the end of the millenium are such as change and cultural shift. The male President of the Norwegian Tourist Association, Torstein Dahle, recently asked: "who will take the responsibility to teach young generations the pleasure of managing with only a little?". Many people, such as some eco-feminist researchers, have claimed that women have a crucial position in the great changes humanity faces. This surely can not be because we are somehow closer to nature than men as a result of our sex, or because our nature is in some way more naturally good than men's. Women might be the significant 'answer' to this question. However, not because of our biology but because of the power relations which exist between women and men, and women's role in society as mothers and teachers. What is imperative is men's recognition of the significance of these personal and global power relations and how they are implicated in global crises and their solutions.

Outdoor adventure, friluftsliv and nature-based sport and education have been, and still are, of great significance culturally and socially both in UK and Norway. Collaboration and exchange of knowledge and ideas within these fields have so far taken place largely between men with little explorations or critical reflexive awareness of mutual male biases. In this paper, we have explored, albeit briefly, some similarities and differences and relationships between outdoor adventure and frilusliv in UK and Norway respectively. Thus we have highlighted some issues that emerge when focusing on gender and especially women's conditions and experiences in the two countries. Further developments of such comparative approach may give interesting new insights into the complexity of relationship between gender, nature and culture. The complex relationships between gender, nature and culture become, however, ever more complex and paradoxical when they are related to the global and increasing ecological crisis and exploitation of nature of which recreationalists and adventurers are not exempt.

Note

1 Friluftsliv is traditionally connected with a practice of simplicity, 'sportsmanship' and travelling through the landscape without leaving traces. The ideology stresses that you are able to carry all the equipment you need in your backpack, even on longer trips. In this tradition, the hike is given central value, either through walking or skiing. There are also the aspects of enjoyment, recreation, aesthetic experiences and a confirmation of national identity.

References

Allin, L. (1998a) this volume.

———(1998b) 'Gender r elations and competence criteria in women's outdoor experiences', in P. Higgins and B. Humberstone (eds) *Celebrating diversity: Learning by sharing cultural differences*. Buckinghamshire: European Institute for Outdoor Adventure Education and Experiential Learning, pp. 41–45.

Allwood, J. *et al.* (eds) (1983) *Naturen som symbol*. Stockholm: Liber Förlag.

Braidotti, R., Charkiewicz, E., Häusler, S. and Wieringa, S. (1994) *Women, the environment and sustainable development*. Women's Research Institute of the United Nations.

Douglas, E. (1998) 'Women, freedom and risk',*Climber* (June): pp. 37–38.

Eder, E. G. (1995) 'Colonisation of open space by sports', in O. Weiss and W. Schulz (eds) *Sport in space and time*. Vienna: Vienna University Press, pp. 43-48.

Hage, T. (ed) (1989) *Kvinner og friluftsliv*. Trondheim: Direktoratet for naturforvaltning.

Humberstone, B. (1986) 'Learning for a change: A study of gender and schooling in outdoor education', in J. Evans (ed) *Physical education, sport and schooling*. London: Falmer Press, pp. 195–214.

———(1996) 'Other voices: Many veanings? T echnique and philosophy for outdoor adventure. The case for women', *Journal of Adventure Education and Outdoor Leadership*, Vol. 14, No. 2: pp. 47–52.

———(1998a) 'Re-cr eation and connections in and with nature: Synthesising ecological and feminist discourses', *The International Review for the Sociology of Sport*, Vol. 33. No. 4. pp. 381–392.

———(1998b) 'Positioning outdoor adventur e education in a postmodern society; Gender relations and outdoor adventure education', in P. Higgins and B. Humberstone (eds) *Celebrating diversity: Learning by sharing cultural differences*. Buckinghamshire: European Institute for Outdoor Adventure Education and Experiential Learning, pp. 46–49.

———(1998c) Theorising Dif ference, Diversity and Emancipation in Sport and Physical Education Cultures, unpublished paper.

———(1999) 'Social exclusion, diversity and equal opportunities: Organisational responses and (re)-actions', in P. Higgins and B. Humberstone (eds) *Outdoor adventure education and experiential learning in the UK*. Luneburg, Germany: Verlag Erlebnispadagogik, pp. 91–95.

Humberstone, B. and Collins, D. (1998) 'Ecofeminism, "Risk" and women's experiences of Landscape', in C. Aitchison and F. Jordan (eds)*Gender, space and identity*. LSA Publication No. 63. Eastbourne: Leisure Studies Association, pp. 137–150.

Humberstone, B. and Lynch, P. (1992) 'Girl's concepts of themselves and their experiences of outdoor education programmes',*Journal of Adventure Education and Outdoor Leadership*, Vol. 8: pp. 27–31.

Humberstone, B. and Pedersen, K. (forthcoming) *A Historical Comparative Analysis of Outdoor Adventure (UK) and Friluftsliv (Norway). The Gendering of 'Natural' Spaces*.

Humberstone, B., Amesberger, G., Becker, P., Bowles, S., Higgins, P., Keus, B., Neuman, J. and Schirp, J. (1998) 'Culture, diversity, national communities and outdoor adventure education', in P. Higgins and B. Humberstone (eds) *Celebrating diversity: Learning by sharing cultural differences*. Buckinghamshire: European Institute for Outdoor Adventure Education and Experiential Learning, pp. 6–8.

Pedersen, K. (1992) 'Friluftsliv og hverdagsliv. Noen foreløpige refleksjoner omkring kvinners og menns ulike vilkår for deltakelse', in Sjong, M. L. (ed.) *Geografi og kjærlighet*. Røros: Skrifter fra Norske Samfunnsgeografers Forening, No. 3: pp. 138-145.

Pedersen, K. (1993a) 'Gender, nature and technology: Changing trends in 'wilderness life' in Northern Norway', in J. Oakes and R. Riewe (eds) *Human ecology: Issues in the North, Volume II*. Edmonton: The Canadian Circumpolar Institute, University of Alberta, pp. 53–66.

Pedersen, K. (1993b) *Kvinneretta opplæring i friluftsliv — perspektiver, utfordringer, erfaringer*. Alta: Alta lærerhøgskole.

Pedersen, K. (1994) 'Wilderness life in women's lives', in Sekretaratet for kvinneforskning (ed.) *Kvinner — En utfordring for idretten?* Oslo: Norwegian Research Council, pp. 139–152.

Pedersen, K. (1995) 'På sporet av et mangfold av friluftslivsstiler', in Damkjær, S. and Ottesen, L. (eds) *Ud i det fri: Sport, friluftsliv, turisme*. Odense: Odense Universitetsforlag.

Pedersen, K. (1997) 'Tracing underlying ideas of masculinity in the Norwegian Traditions of friluftsliv'. Paper presented at the International Conference for the Sociology of Sport, Oslo.

Pedersen, K. (1998a) 'Doing feminist ethnography in the wilderness around my home town: Methodological reflections', *International Review for the Sociology of Sport*, Vol. 33. No. 4: pp. 393–402.

Pedersen, K. (1998b) 'Globalization of local culture? A study of "wilderness" experiences and changes in women's lives in Alta, Northern Norway', Paper prepared for the 14th World Congress of Sociology, July 26th-August 1st, Montreal, Canada.

Pedersen, K. (1998c) 'Friluftsliv viewed from the top of Europe', in P. Higgins and B. Humberstone (eds) *Celebrating diversity: Learning by sharing cultural differences*. Buckinghamshire: European Institute for Outdoor Adventure Education and Experiential Learning, pp. 24–30.

Price, M. (1996) *People and tourism in fragile environments*. London: John Wiley & sSon.

Ryall, A. (1985) 'Odyssavs i skjørt', in *Nytt om Kvinneforskning* No. 2: pp. 3–9.

Salleh, A. (1997) *Ecofeminism as politics, nature, Marx and the postmodern*. London: Zen Books.

Thompson, S. M. (1997) For love not money: Gendered labour in sporting cultures. Keynote paper presented at the symposium of International Sociology of Sport Association. 28th June — 1st July, Norway.

Warren, K. (ed)(1996) *Women's voices in experiential education*. Dubuque, IA: Kendal/Hunt Pub. Co.

Weeks, J. (1993) 'Rediscovering values', in J. Squires (ed) *Principled positions*. London: Lawrence and Wishart.

Williams, R. (1976) *Nature. Key-words: A vocabulary of society and nature*. London: Fontana.

Williams, R. (1988) *Keywords: A Vocabulary of culture and society*. London: Fontana

About the Contributors

STEPHEN J. ALBRECHTSEN is Director of the Human Performance Laboratory and Professor of Health, Physical Education, Recreation and Coaching at the University of Wisconsin—Whitewater. He received his doctoral degree from Colorado State University and has held teaching and administrative appointments at Colorado State University and the University of Colorado in addition to the University of Wisconsin—Whitewater. His recent research and professional activities have included the promotion of opportunities to improve health through active life-styles and leisure. His professional affiliations include the American Alliance for Health, Physical Education, Recreation and Dance, the American College of Sports Medicine, and the World Leisure and Recreation Association. He is a frequent speaker for professional organizations at national and international conferences.

LINDA ALLIN is a Lecturer in the Division of Sport Sciences at the University of Northumbria at Newcastle, where her teaching areas include the sociology of sport and outdoor fieldwork experiences. Her current research interests focus on a PhD concerning the construction of women's career identities in outdoor education. Linda has kayaked in India, Nepal, Austria, France and the UK. She is women's representative for the British Canoe Union Northern Region and has worked seasonally in a variety of outdoor centres. Nowadays she is often to be found in a wetsuit, taking turns with her husband in kayaking and pushing a pram around the Tees Barrage white water site.

KAREN L. BARAK obtained her baccalaureate degree in Recreation Leadership and masters degree in College Student Personnel from the University of Wisconsin–LaCrosse, and her doctorate in Educational Administration with a focus on Higher Education from the University of Wisconsin–Madison. Previously, she was employed by the University of Wisconsin–Oshkosh in Residence Life for Leadership Development in Residence Hall Government, by the Girl Scouts of the United States of America for adult education, and by the University of Wisconsin–Madison in Campus Activities. Karen's research has focused on developmental issues of college students, experiential education, and administration. Her publications have included those on instructional techniques and course content, student learning, and adventure education. She has also made presentations to World Leisure and Recreation Association, Wisconsin Park and Recreation Association, American Camping Association, and Association for Worksite Health Promotion.

MAY CARTER spent much of her childhood exploring the local bushland and playing in the creek with her twin brother and all the boys in her street. In her early twenties, she deviated from her safe and secure career path as a medical secretary to pursue employment outdoors. She has now been involved in adventure recreation and education for almost fifteen years, including five years running an adventure recreation business, Everybody's Game. May developed an interest in women and leadership in adventure recreation and is currently completing a Master of Social Science (Leisure Sciences) degree at Edith Cowan University in Western Australia.

DI COLLINS was formerly a primary school teacher, later a youth and community educator, and is currently working as a researcher, facilitator and consultant. She values the experience of the outdoors for its potential for holistic learning, with its spatial and temporal separation and opportunities for reflection and objectivity, and personal, group and organisational development. In her work, Di has found that in developing a relationship with each other, group members also developed a heightened awareness of the environment. The development of confidence in outdoor skills was often associated with a growth in self-esteem, and this became the focus of her Master's dissertation. Di is also currently a part-time M.Phil./Ph.D. research student at Buckinghamshire Chilterns University College.

TONY CURSON is Head of School of Leisure, Tourism and Hospitality Management at the University of North London (UNL). His teaching and research interests are in leisure policy and planning and leisure and local governance. He also has a particular interest in urban recreation, having undertaken studies of the use of parks and open space for The Royal Parks Agency and London Boroughs. At the time of writing (September 1999), he is engaged in a study of open space planning in London for the London Planning Advisory Committee. Prior to joining UNL, tony worked for 10 years as Principal Recreation Planner for Milton Keynes Development Corporation where he was responsible for research, policy, planning and project management, including the development of the City's parks and open space system. Tony has also worked for six years in local government in leisure research and policy.

MARY ANNE HEDRICH Holds an undergraduate degree in nursing from the University of Michigan, a masters degree in health education and a doctoral degree in curriculum and instruction with foci in health education, preventive medicine and human relations from The University of Wisconsin—Madison. She has taught at Carroll College and the University of Wisconsin— Whitewater with major interests in the role of self esteem in learning, dealing with differences, and conflict resolution utilizing experiential education methodology. As director of a camp for boys and girls aged 8 through 17 years, Mary Anne developed programming that promoted positive self-esteem, with adventure activities as the primary facilitating element. Her research and publications in self/other concept and self/other esteem of adolescents, maximizing learning, and dealing with differences reflect those interests. She has presented at the Critical Thinking and Educational Reform and The Society for the Scientific Study of Sexuality international conferences.

BARBARA HUMBERSTONE is Reader in critical sociology of outdoor educa- tion, leisure and sport at Buckinghamshire Chilterns University College, Buckinghamshire, UK. She supervises research into outdoor education and other areas of leisure and sport. She has written widely on equity, equal opportunities and outdoor education and is particularly interested in the relations between environmental and social justice. She was secretary of the Association for Outdoor Learning (AfOL) (formally NAOE) for a number of years and is currently its co-ordinator for further and higher education and research. She is a board member of the European Institute for Outdoor Adventure Education and Experiential Learning. Her leisure interests include windsurfing, walking and climbing.

CLARE KITTS is a Senior Lecturer in Leisure Management at the University of North London. Her teaching and research interests focus on outdoor sport and leisure management and international sports policy. Prior to joining the University, Clare managed a water sports centre and public park which attracted a diversity of users. Her current research project aims to study the perceptions of sports spaces of urban and rural school children.

KIRSTI PEDERSON is Associate Professor in physical education and sport studies at Finnmark College, Norway. She is educated as a primary school teacher as well as a physical education teacher, and holds a master's degree in sports (her thesis was written on women's movement cultures). Her contribution in this publication is based on her currently released PhD which is an anthropological approach to the study of outdoor recreation and adventure among women living in the very North of Norway. She has been teaching outdoor adventure, dance, and teaching methods and methodology in higher education since 1980.

VAL WOODWARD IS Lecturer in Community Work University of Plymouth, and was previously community work lecturer at University of Strathclyde. Before that — community worker with Lothian Regional Council, and a local voluntary group in Edinburgh. She teaches windsurfing part time, including running a Women's evening at Siblyback Lake in Cornwall. Val is politically active, for example chairing the Women's Committee at Edinburgh District Council in the 1980s. This article brings together her various academic and practice interests.

Other LSA Publications Volumes

The list is chronological (generally in order of publication date). Volumes 1–47 are A4 format, published 1976–1992. More recent volumes from No. 48 on are 6x9 inch, paperback. Prices vary according to LSA membership status. Orders/information may be obtained from: LSA PUBLICATIONS c/o The Chelsea School, University of Brighton, Eastbourne BN20 7SP (UK)FAX (0044) (0)1323 644641 or E-mail: mcfee@solutions-inc.co.uk

For more information on newest volumes, please contact LSA Publications.

LEISURE, TIME AND SPACE:
MEANINGS AND VALUES IN PEOPLE'S LIVES

LSA Publication No. 57. ISBN: 0 906337 68 2 [1998] pp. 198 + iv
Edited by Sheila Scraton

Contents